PANOPTICON; OR, THE INSPECTION-HOUSE:

CONTAINING THE IDEA OF A NEW PRINCIPLE OF
CONSTRUCTION APPLICABLE TO ANY SORT OF
ESTABLISHMENT, IN WHICH PERSONS OF ANY DESCRIPTION
ARE TO BE KEPT UNDER INSPECTION; AND IN PARTICULAR
TO PENITENTIARY-HOUSES, PRISONS, HOUSES OF INDUSTRY,
WORK-HOUSES, POOR-HOUSES, LAZARETTOS,
MANUFACTORIES, HOSPITALS, MAD-HOUSES, AND SCHOOLS:
WITH A PLAN OF MANAGEMENT ADAPTED TO THE
PRINCIPLE:

IN A SERIES OF LETTERS, WRITTEN IN THE YEAR 1787, FROM
CRECHEFF IN WHITE RUSSIA. TO A FRIEND IN ENGLAND

BY JEREMY BENTHAM, OF LINCOLN'S INN, ESQUIRE.

CONTENTS

Preface

Morals reformed—health preserved—industry invigorated—instruction diffused—public burthens lightened—Economy seated, as it were, upon a rock—the gordian knot of the Poor-Laws not cut, but untied—all by a simple idea in Architecture!—Thus much I ventured to say on laying down the pen—and thus much I should perhaps have said on taking it up, if at that early period I had seen the whole of the way before me. A new mode of obtaining power of mind over mind, in a quantity hitherto without example: and that, to a degree equally without example, secured by whoever chooses to have it so, against abuse.—Such is the engine: such the work that may be done with it. How far the expectations thus held out have been fulfilled, the reader will decide.

The Letters which compose the body of this tract were written at Crecheff in Russia, and from thence sent to England in the year 1787, much about the same time with the Defence of Usury. They were addressed to a particular person, with a view to a particular establishment then in contemplation (intelligence of which had found its way to me through the medium of an English newspaper), and without any immediate or very determinate view to general publication. The attention of the public in Ireland having been drawn to one of the subjects to which they relate, by the notice given not long ago by the Chancellor of the Exchequer, of a disposition on the part of government there, to make trial of the Penitentiary system, it is on that account that they now see the light through the medium of the Irish press.

They are printed as at first written, with no other alteration than the erasure of a few immaterial passages, and the addition of a Postscript, stating such new ideas as have been the fruit of a more detailed and critical examination, undertaken chiefly with an eye to the particular establishment last mentioned, and assisted by professional information and advice.

In running over the descriptive part of the letters, the reader will find it convenient to remember, that alterations, as stated in the Postscript, have been made, though he need not at that period trouble himself with considering what they are: since in either shape the details will serve equally well for the illustration of the general principle, and for the proof of the advantages that may be derived from it.

In what concerns the Penitentiary system, I may be observed to have discussed, with rather more freedom than may perhaps be universally acceptable, a variety of measures either established or proposed by gentlemen who have laboured in the same line. A task this, which I would gladly have avoided: but complete justice could not otherwise have been done to the plan here proposed, nor its title to preference placed in a satisfactory point of view. Among the notions thus treated, it is with pleasure rather than regret that I observe several which on a former occasion I had myself either suggested or subscribed to. I say with pleasure: regarding the incident as a proof of my having no otherwise done by others than as I not only would be done by, but have actually done by myself: a consideration which will, I hope, make my apology to the respectable gentlemen concerned, and assist their candour in recommending me to their forgiveness. If by the light of reciprocal animadversion I should find myself enabled to rectify any errors of my own which may still have escaped me, the correction, instead of being shrunk from as a punishment, will be embraced as a reward.

In point of method and compression, something might have been gained, had the whole, Letters and Postscript together, been new cast, and the supplemental matter worked up with the original. But time was wanting; and, if the invention be worth any thing, the account given of it will not be the less amusing or less instructive, for being exhibited in an historical and progressive point of view.

The concluding Letter on Schools is a sort of *jeu d'esprit*, which would hardly have presented itself in so light a form, at any other period than at the moment of conception, and under the flow of spirits which the charms of novelty are apt enough to inspire. As such, it may possibly help to alleviate the tedium of a dry discussion, and on that score obtain the pardon, should it fail of receiving the approbation, of the graver class of readers.

Panopticon; or, The Inspection-House

Letter I.: Idea of the Inspection Principle.

Crecheff in White Russia, -1787.

Dear * * * *,—I observed t'other day in one of your English papers, an advertisement relative to a House of Correction therein spoken of, as intended for * * * * * * *. It occurred to me, that the plan of a building, lately contrived by my brother, for purposes in some respects similar, and which, under the name of the *Inspection House*, or the *Elaboratory*, he is about erecting here, might afford some hints for the above establishment. I have accordingly obtained some drawings relative to it, which I here inclose. Indeed I look upon it as capable of applications of the most extensive nature; and that for reasons which you will soon perceive.

To say all in one word, it will be found applicable, I think, without exception, to all establishments whatsoever, in which, within a space not too large to be covered or commanded by buildings, a number of persons are meant to be kept under inspection. No matter how different, or even opposite the purpose: whether it be that of *punishing the incorrigible, guarding the insane, reforming the vicious, confining the suspected, employing the idle, maintaining the helpless, curring the sick, instructing the willing* in any branch of industry, or *training the rising race* in the path of *education*: in a word, whether it be applied to the purposes of *perpetual prisons* in the room of death, or *prisons for confinement* before trial, or *penitentiary-houses*, or *houses of correction*, or *work-houses*, or *manufactories*, or *mad-houses*, or *hospitals*, or *schools*.

It is obvious that, in all these instances, the more constantly the persons to be inspected are under the eyes of the persons who should inspect them, the more perfectly will the purpose of the establishment have been attained. Ideal perfection, if that were the object, would require that each person should actually be in that predicament, during every instant of time. This being impossible, the next thing to be wished for is, that, at every instant, seeing reason to believe as much, and not being able to satisfy himself to the contrary, he should *conceive* himself to be so. This point, you will immediately see, is most completely secured by my brother's plan; and, I think, it will appear equally manifest, that it cannot be compassed by any other, or to speak more properly, that if it be compassed by any other, it can only be in proportion as such other may approach to this.

To cut the matter as short as possible, I will consider it at once in its application to such purposes as, being most complicated, will serve to exemplify the greatest force and variety of precautionary contrivance. Such are those which have suggested the idea of *penitentiary-houses*: in which the objects of *safe custody, confinement, solitude, forced labour,* and *instruction,* were all of them to be kept in view. If all these objects can be accomplished together, of course with at least equal certainty and facility may any lesser number of them.

Letter II.: Plan For a Penitentiary Inspection-house.

Before you look at the plan, take in words the general idea of it.

The building is circular.

The apartments of the prisoners occupy the circumference. You may call them, if you please, the *cells*.

These *cells* are divided from one another, and the prisoners by that means secluded from all communication with each other, by *partitions* in the form of radii issuing from the circumference towards the centre, and extending as many feet as shall be thought necessary to form the largest dimension of the cell.

The apartment of the inspector occupies the centre; you may call it if you please the inspector's *lodge*.

It will be convenient in most, if not in all cases, to have a vacant space or *area* all round, between such centre and such circumference. You may call it if you please the *intermediate* or *annular area*.

About the width of a cell may be sufficient for a *passage* from the outside of the building to the lodge.

Each cell has in the outward circumference, a *window*, large enough, not only to light the cell, but, through the cell, to afford light enough to the correspondent part of the lodge.

The inner circumference of the cell is formed by an iron *grating*, so light as not to screen any part of the cell from the inspector's view.

Of this grating, a part sufficiently large opens, in form of a *door*, to admit the prisoner at his first entrance; and to give admission at any time to the inspector or any of his attendants.

To cut off from each prisoner the view of every other, the partitions are carried on a few feet beyond the grating into the intermediate area. such projecting parts I call the *protracted partitions*.

It is conceived, that the light, coming in in this manner through the cells, and so across the intermediate area, will be sufficient for the inspector's lodge. But, for this purpose, both the windows in the cells, and those corresponding to them in the lodge, should be as large as the strength of the building, and what shall be deemed a necessary attention to economy, will permit.

To the windows of the lodge there are blinds, as high up as the eyes of the prisoners in their cells can, by any means they can employ, be made to reach.

To prevent *thorough light*, whereby, notwithstanding the blinds, the prisoners would see from the cells whether or no any person was in the lodge, that apartment is divided into quarters, by *partitions* formed by two diameters to the circle, crossing each other at right angles. For these partitions the thinnest materials might serve; and they might be made removeable at pleasure; their height, sufficient to prevent the prisoners seeing over them from the cells. Doors to these partitions, if left open at any time, might produce the thorough light. To prevent this, divide each partition into two, at any part required, setting down the one-half at such distance from the other as shall be equal to the apperture of a door.

These windows of the inspector's lodge open into the intermediate area, in the form of *doors*, in as many places as shall be deemed necessary to admit of his communicating readily with any of the cells.

Small *lamps*, in the outside of each window of the lodge, backed by a reflector, to throw the light into the corresponding cells, would extend to the night the security of the day.

To save the troublesome exertion of voice that might otherwise be necessary, and to prevent one prisoner from knowing that the inspector was occupied by another prisoner at a distance, a small *tin tube* might reach from each cell to the inspector's lodge, passing across the area, and so in at the side of the correspondent window of the lodge. By means of this implement, the slightest whisper of the one might be heard by the other, especially if he had proper notice to apply his ear to the tube.

With regard to *instruction*, in cases where it cannot be duly given without the instructor's being close to the work, or without setting his hand to it by way of example before the learner's face, the instructor must indeed here as elsewhere, shift his station as often as there is occasion to visit different workmen; unless he calls the workmen to him, which in some of the instances to which this sort of building is applicable, such as that of imprisoned felons, could not so well be. But in all cases where directions, given verbally and at a distance, are sufficient, these tubes will be found of use. They will save, on the one hand, the exertion of voice it would require, on the part of the instructor, to communicate instruction to the workmen without quitting his central station in the lodge; and, on the other, the confusion which would ensue if different instructors or persons in the lodge were calling to the cells at the same time. And, in the case of hospitals, the quiet that may be insured by this little contrivance, trifling as it may seem at first sight, affords an additional advantage.

A *bell*, appropriated exclusively to the purposes of alarm, hangs in a belfry with which the building is crowned, communicating by a rope with the inspector's lodge.

The most economical, and perhaps the most convenient, way of *warming* the cells and area, would be by flues surrounding it, upon the principle of those in hot-houses. A total want of every means of producing artificial heat might, in such weather as we sometimes have in England, be fatal to the lives of the prisoners; at any rate, it would often times be altogether incompatible with their working at any sedentary employment. The flues, however, and the fire-places belonging to them, instead of being on the outside, as in hot-houses, should be in the inside. By this means, there would be less waste of heat, and the current of air that would rush in on all sides through the cells, to supply the draught made by the fires, would answer so far the purpose of ventilation. But of this more under the head of Hospitals.*

Letter III.: Extent For a Single Building.

So far as to the characteristic parts of the principle of construction. You may now, perhaps, be curious to know to what extent a building upon this principle is capable of being carried, consistently with the various purposes to which it may come to be applied. Upon this subject, to speak with confidence belongs only to architects by profession. Indulge me, however, with a few words at a venture.

As to the *cells*, they will of course be more or less spacious, according to the employment which it is designed should be carried on in them.

As to the *whole building*, if it be too small, the circumference will not be large enough to afford a sufficient number of cells: if too large, the depth from the exterior windows will be too great; and there will not be light enough in the lodge.

As to this individual building of my brother's, the dimensions of it were determined by the consideration of the most convenient scantlings of the timbers, (that being in his situation the cheapest material,) and by other local considerations. It is to have two stories, and the diameter of the whole building is to be 100 feet out and out.

Merely to help conception, I will take this size for an example of such a building as he would propose for England.

Taking the diameter 100 feet, this admits of 48 cells, 6 feet wide each at the outside, walls included; with a *passage* through the building, of 8 or 9 feet.

I begin with supposing two stories of cells.

In the *under* story, thickness of the walls 2½ feet.

From thence, clear *depth* of each cell from the window to the grating, 13 feet.

From thence to the ends of the partition walls, 3 feet more; which gives the length of the *protracted partitions*.

Breadth of the *intermediate area*, 14.

Total from the outside of the building to the *lodge*, 32½ feet.

The double of this, 65 feet, leaves for the *diameter of the lodge*, 35 feet; including the thickness of its walls.

In the *upper* story, the cells will be but 9 feet deep; the difference between that and the 13 feet, which is their depth in the under story, being taken up by a *gallery* which surrounds the protracted partitions.

This gallery supplies, in the upper story, the place of an intermediate area on that floor; and by means of *steps*, which I shall come to presently, forms the communication between the upper story of cells to which it is attached, and the lower story of the cells, together with the intermediate area and the lodge.

The spot most remote from the place where the light comes in from, I mean the *centrical* spot of the building and of the lodge, will not be more than 50 feet distant from that place; a distance not greater, I imagine, than what is often times exemplified in churches; even in such as are not furnished in the manner of this building, with *windows* in every part of the exterior boundary. But the inspector's windows will not be more than about 32½ feet from the open light.

It would be found convenient, I believe, on many accounts, and in most instances, to make *one story* of the *lodge* serve for *two stories* of the *cells*; especially in any situation where ground is valuable, the number of persons to be inspected large, the room necessary for each person not very considerable, and frugality and necessity more attended to than appearance.

For this purpose, the *floor* of the *ground story of the lodge* is elevated to within about 4½ feet of the floor of the first story of the cells. By this means, the inspector's eye, when he stands up, will be on, or a little above, the level of the floor of the above mentioned upper story of the cells; and, at any rate, he will command both that and the ground story of the cells without difficulty, and without change of posture.

As to the *intermediate area*, the *floor* of it is upon a level, not with the *floor* of the lodge, but with that of the *lower story* of the cells. But at the *upper story* of the cells, its place, as I have already mentioned, is supplied by the above-mentioned *gallery*; so that the altitude of this area from the floor to the ceiling is equal to that of both stories of the cells put together.

The floor of the lodge not being on a level with either story of the cells, but between both, it must at convenient intervals be provided with flights of *steps*, to go *down* to the ground story of the cells by the intermediate area, and *up* to the first floor of the cells by the gallery. The ascending flights, joined to the *descending*, enable the servants of the house to go to the upper story of the cells, without passing through the apartment of the inspector.

As to the *height* of the whole, and of the several parts, it is supposed that 18 feet might serve for the *two stories of cells*, to be inspected, as above, by *one story* of the *lodge*. This would hold 96 persons.

36 feet for four stories of *cells*, and two of the lodge: this would hold 192 persons.

54 feet for six stories of the cells, and three of the lodge: this would hold 288 persons.

And 54 feet, it is conceived, would not be an immoderate elevation.

The drawings which, I believe, will accompany this, suppose *four* for the number of stories of the cells.

You will see, under the head of hospitals, the reasons why I conceive that even a less height than 9 feet, deducting the thickness of a floor supported by arches, might be sufficient for the cells.

The *passage* might have, for its *height*, either the height of one story, or of two stories of the cells, according as the number of those cells was two or four. The part over the passage might, in either case, be added to the lodge, to which it would thereby give a communication, at each end, with the world without doors, and ensure a keeper against the danger of finding himself a prisoner among his prisoners.

Should it be thought, that, in this way, the lodge would not have light enough, for the convenience of a man of a station competent to the office, the deficiency might be supplied by a void space left in that part, all the way up. You may call it if you please the central area. Into this space windows may open where they are wanted, from the apartments of the lodge. It may be either left open at the top, or covered with a *sky-light*. But this expedient, though it might add, in some respects, to the convenience of the lodge, could not but add considerably to the quantity and expense of the building.

On the other hand, it would be assistant to ventilation. Here, too, would be a proper place for the *chapel*: the prisoners remaining in their cells, and the windows of the lodge, which is almost all window, being thrown open. The advantages derivable from it in point of light and ventilation depending upon its being kept vacant, it can never be wanted for any profane use. It may therefore, with the greater propriety, be allotted to divine service, and receive a regular consecration. The *pulpit* and *sounding-board* may be moveable. During the term of service, the sky-light, at all other times kept as open as possible, might be shut.

Letter IV.: The Principle Extended to Uncovered Areas.

In my two last letters, I gave you such idea as it was in my power to give you by words, of this new plan of construction, considered in its most simple form. A few more with regard to what further *extensions* it may admit of.

The utmost number of persons that could be stowed in a single building of this sort, consistently with the purposes of each several institution, being ascertained, to increase the number, that of the buildings must of course be increased. Suppose *two* of these *rotundas* requisite: these two might, *by a covered gallery* constructed upon the same principles, be consolidated into one inspection-house. And by the help of such a covered gallery, *the field of inspection* might be dilated to any extent.

If the number of rotundas were extended to *four*, a regular uncovered area might in that way be inclosed; and being surrounded by covered galleries, would be commanded in this manner from all sides, instead of being commanded only from one.

The area thus inclosed might be either *circular* like the buildings, or *square*, or *oblong*, as one or other of those forms were best adapted to the prevailing ideas of beauty or local convenience. A chain of any length, composed of inspection-houses adapted to the same or different purposes, might in this way be carried round an area of any extent.

On such a plan, either one inspector might serve for two or more rotundas, or if there were one to each, *the inspective force*, if I may use the expression, would be greater in such a compound building, than in any of the number singly taken, of which it was composed; since each inspector might be relieved occasionally by every other.

In the uncovered area thus brought within the field of inspection, out-door employments, or any employments requiring a greater covered space than the general form of construction will allow, might be carried on upon the same principle. A kitchen-garden might then be cultivated for the use of the whole society, by a few members of it at a time, to whom such an opportunity of airing and exercising themselves would be a refreshment and indulgence.

Many writers have expatiated with great force and justice, on the unpopular and unedifying cast of that undistinguishing discipline, which, in situation and treatment, confounds the lot of those who *may* prove innocent, with the lot of those who *have been* proved to be guilty. The same roof, it has been said, ought not to inclose persons who stand in predicaments so dissimilar. In a combination of inspection-houses, this delicacy might be observed without any abatement of that vigilance with regard to safe custody, which in both cases is equally indispensable.

Letter V.: Essential Points of the Plan.

It may be of use, that among all the particulars you have seen, it should be clearly understood what circumstances are, and what are not, essential to the plan. The essence of it consists, then, in the *centrality* of the inspector's situation, combined with the wellknown and most effectual contrivances for *seeing without being seen*. As to the *general form* of the building, the most commodious for most purposes seems to be the circular: but this is not an absolutely essential circumstance. Of all figures, however, this, you will observe, is the only one that affords a perfect view, and the same view, of an indefinite number of apartments of the same dimensions: that affords a spot from which, without any change of situation, a man may survey, in the same perfection, the whole number, and without so much as a change of posture, the half of the whole number, at the same time: that, within a boundary of a given extent, contains the greatest quantity of room:—that places the centre at the least distance from the light:—that gives the cells most width, at the part where, on account of the light, most light may, for the purposes of work, be wanted:—and that reduces to the greatest possible shortness the path taken by the inspector, in passing from each part of the field of inspection to every other.

You will please to observe, that though perhaps it is the most important point, that the persons to be inspected should always feel themselves as if under inspection, at least as standing a great chance of being so, yet it is not by any means the *only* one. If it were, the same advantage might be given to buildings of almost any form. What is also of importance is, that for the greatest proportion of time possible, each man should actually *be* under inspection. This is material in *all* cases, that the inspector may have the satisfaction of knowing, that the discipline actually has the effect which it is designed to have: and it is more particularly material in such cases where the inspector, besides seeing that they conform to such standing rules as are prescribed, has more or less frequent occasion to give them such transient and incidental directions as will require to be given and enforced, at the commencement at least of every course of industry. And I think, it needs not much argument to prove, that the business of inspection, like every other, will be performed to a greater degree of perfection, the less trouble the performance of it requires.

Not only so, but the greater chance there is, of a given person's being at a given time actually under inspection, the more strong will be the persuasion—the more *intense*, if I may say so, the *feeling*, he has of his being so. How little turn soever the greater number of persons so circumstanced may be supposed to have for calculation, some rough sort of calculation can scarcely, under such circumstances, avoid forcing itself upon the rudest mind. Experiment, venturing first upon slight trangressions, and so on, in proportion to success, upon more and more considerable ones, will not fail to teach him the difference between a loose inspection and a strict one.

It is for these reasons, that I cannot help looking upon every form as less and less eligible, in proportion as it deviates from the *circular*.

A very material point is, that room be allotted to the lodge sufficient to adapt it to the purpose of a complete and constant habitation for the principal inspector or headkeeper, and his family. The more numerous also the family, the better; since, by this means, there will in fact be as many inspectors, as the family consists of persons, though only one be paid for it. Neither the orders of the inspector himself, nor any interest which they may feel, or not feel, in the regular performance of his duty, would be requisite to find them motives adequate to the purpose. Secluded oftentimes, by their situation, from every other object, they will naturally, and in a manner unavoidably, give their eyes a direction conformable to that purpose, in every momentary interval of their ordinary occupations. It will supply in their instance the place of that great and constant fund of entertainment to the sedentary and vacant in towns—the looking out of the window. The scene, though a confined, would be a very various, and therefore, perhaps, not altogether an unamusing one.

Letter VI.: Advantages of the Plan.

I flatter myself there can now be little doubt of the plan's possessing the fundamental advantages I have been attributing to it: I mean, the *apparent omnipresence* of the inspector (if divines will allow me the expression,) combined with the extreme facility of his *real presence*.

A collateral advantage it possesses, and on the score of frugality a very material one, is that which respects the *number* of the inspectors requisite. If this plan required more than another, the additional number would form an objection, which, were the difference to a certain degree considerable, might rise so high as to be conclusive: so far from it, that a greater multitude than ever were yet lodged in one house might be inspected by a single person; for the trouble of inspection is diminished in no less proportion than the strictness of inspection is increased.

Another very important advantage, whatever purposes the plan may be applied to, particularly where it is applied to the severest and most coercive purposes, is, that the *under* keepers or inspectors, the servants and subordinates of every kind, will be under the same irresistible controul with respect to the *head* keeper or inspector, as the prisoners or other persons to be governed are with respect to *them*. On the common plans, what means, what possibility, has the prisoner, of appealing to the humanity of the principal for redress against the neglect or oppression of subordinates in that rigid sphere, but the *few* opportunities which, in a crowded prison, the most conscientious keeper *can* afford—but the none at all which many a keeper *thinks* fit to give them? How different would their lot be upon this plan!

In no instance could his subordinates either perform or depart from their duty, but he must know the time and degree and manner of their doing so. It presents an answer, and that a satisfactory one, to one of the most puzzling of political questions—*quis custodiet ipsos custodes?* And, as the fulfilling of his, as well as their, duty would be rendered so much easier, than it can ever have been hitherto, so might, and so should, any departure from it be punished with the more inflexible severity. It is this circumstance that renders the influence of this plan not less beneficial to what is called *liberty*, than to necessary coercion; not less powerful as a controul upon subordinate power, than as a curb to delinquency; as a shield to innocence, than as a scourge to guilt.

Another advantage, still operating to the same ends, is the great load of trouble and disgust which it takes off the shoulders of those occasional inspectors of a higher order, such as *judges* and other *magistrates*, who, called down to this irksome task from the superior ranks of life, cannot but feel a proportionable repugnance to the discharge of it. Think how it is with them upon the present plans, and how it still must be upon the best plans that have been hitherto devised! The cells or apartments, however constructed, must, if there be nine hundred of them (as there were to have been upon the penitentiary-house plan,) be opened to the visitors, one by one. To do their business to any purpose, they must approach near to, and come almost in contact with each inhabitant; whose situation being watched over according to no other than the loose methods of inspection at present practicable, will on that account require the more minute and troublesome investigation on the part of these occasional superintendents. By this new plan, the disgust is entirely removed, and the trouble of going into such a room as the lodge, is no more than the trouble of going into any other.

Were *Newgate* upon this plan, all Newgate might be inspected by a quarter of an hour's visit to Mr. Akerman.

Among the other causes of that reluctance, none at present so forcible, none so unhappily well grounded, none which affords so natural an excuse, nor so strong a reason against accepting of any excuse, as the danger of *infection*—a circumstance which carries death, in one of its most tremendous forms, from the seat of guilt to the seat of justice, involving in one common catastrophe the violator and the upholder of the laws. But in a spot so constructed, and under a course of discipline so insured, how should infection ever arise? or how should it continue? Against every danger of this kind, what private house of the poor, one might almost say, or even of the most opulent, can be equally secure?

Nor is the disagreeableness of the task of superintendence diminished by this plan, in a much greater degree than the efficacy of it is increased. On all others, be the superintendent's visit ever so unexpected, and his motions ever so quick, time there must always be for preparations blinding the real state of things. Out of nine hundred cells, he can visit but one at a time, and, in the meanwhile, the worst of the others may be arranged, and the inhabitants threatened, and tutored how to receive him. On this plan, no sooner is the superintendent announced, than the whole scene opens instantaneously to his view.

In mentioning inspectors and superintendents who are such by office, I must not overlook that system of inspection, which, however little heeded, will not be the less useful and efficacious: I mean, the part which individuals may be disposed to take in the business, without intending, perhaps, or even without thinking of, any other effects of their visits, than the gratification of their own particular curiosity. What the inspector's or keeper's family are with respect to *him*, that, and more, will these spontaneous visitors be to the superintendent, —assistants, deputies, in so far as he is faithful, witnesses and judges, should he ever be unfaithful, to his trust. So as they are but there, what the motives were that drew them thither is perfectly immaterial; whether the relieving of their anxieties by the affecting prospect of their respective friends and relatives thus detained in durance, or merely the satisfying that general curiosity, which an establishment, on various accounts so interesting to human feelings, may naturally be expected to excite.

You see, I take for granted as a matter of course, that under the necessary regulations for preventing interruption and disturbance, the doors of these establishments will be, as, without very special reasons to the contrary, the doors of all public establishments ought to be, thrown wide open to the body of the curious at large—the great open committee of the tribunal of the world. And who ever objects to such publicity, where it is practicable, but those whose motives for objection afford the strongest reasons for it?

Letter VII.: Penitentiary-houses—safe Custody.

Decomposing the plan, I will now take the liberty of offering a few separate considerations, applicable to the different purposes to which it appears capable of being applied.

A *Penitentiary-house*, more particularly is (I am sorry I must correct myself, and say, was to have been) what every prison might, and in some degree at least ought to be, designed at once as a place of *safe custody*, and a place of *labour*. Every such place must necessarily be, whether designed or not, an *hospital*—a place where sickness will be found at least, whether provision be or be not made for its relief. I will consider this plan in its application to these three distinguishable purposes.

Against *escapes*, and in particular on the part of felons of every description, as well before as after conviction, persons from the desperateness of whose situation attempts to escape are more particularly to be apprehended, it would afford, as I dare say you see already, a degree of security, which, perhaps, has been scarce hitherto reached by conception, much less by practice. Overpowering the guard requires an union of hands, and a concert among minds. But what union, or what concert, can there be among persons, no one of whom will have set eyes on any other from the first moment of his entrance? Undermining walls, forcing iron bars, requires commonly a concert, always a length of time exempt from interruption. But who would think of beginning a work of hours and days, without any tolerable prospect of making so much as the first motion towards it unobserved? Such attempts have been seldom made without the assistance of implements introduced by accomplices from without. But who would expose themselves even to the slightest punishment, or even to the mortification of the disappointment, without so much as a tolerable chance of escaping instantaneous detection?—Who would think of bringing in before the keeper's face, so much as a small file, or a phial of *aqua fortis*, to a person not prepared to receive any such thing, nor in a condition to make use of it? Upon all plans hitherto pursued, the thickest walls have been found occasionally unavailing: upon this plan, the thinnest would be sufficient—a circumstance which must operate, in a striking degree, towards a diminution of the expense.

In this, as in every other application of the plan, you will find its lenient, not less conspicuous than its coercive, tendency; insomuch that, if you were to be asked who had most cause to wish for its adoption, you might find yourself at some loss to determine between the malefactors themselves, and those for whose sake they are consigned to punishment.

In this view I am sure you cannot overlook the effect which it would have in rendering unnecessary that inexhaustible fund of disproportionate, too often needless, and always unpopular severity, not to say torture—the use of *irons*. Confined in one of these cells, every motion of the limbs, and every muscle of the face exposed to view, what pretence could there be for exposing to this hardship the most boisterous malefactor? Indulged with perfect liberty within the space allotted to him, in what worse way could he vent his rage, than by beating his head against the walls? and who but himself would be a sufferer by such folly? Noise, the only offence by which a man thus engaged could render himself troublesome (an offence, by the bye, against which irons themselves afford no security,) might, if found otherwise incorrigible, be subdued by *gagging*—a most natural and efficacious mode of prevention, as well as punishment, the prospect of which would probably be for ever sufficient to render the infliction of it unnecessary. Punishment, even in its most hideous forms, loses its odious character, when bereft of that *uncertainty*, without which the rashest desperado would not expose himself to its stroke. If an instance be wanted, think what the means are, which the so much admired law of England makes use of, and that in one of its most admired branches, to work, not upon criminals, but upon its favourite class of judges? what but death? and that no common death, but death the slow but necessary result of lingering torture. And yet, whatever other reproach the law may be thought to merit, in what instance was it ever seen to expose itself in this way to the reproach of cruelty?

Letter VIII.: Uses—penitentiary-houses—reformation.

In my last, I endeavoured to state to you the advantages which a receptacle, upon the plan of the proposed building, seemed to promise in its application to places of *confinement*, considered merely in that view. Give me leave now to consider it as applicable to the joint purposes of *punishment, reformation*, and *pecuniary economy*.

That in regard to persons of the description of those to whom punishments of the nature in question are destined, solitude is in its nature subservient to the purpose of reformation, seems to be as little disputed, as its tendency to operate in addition to the mass of sufferance. But that upon this plan that purpose would be effected, at least as completely as it could be on any other, you cannot but see at the first glance, or rather you must have observed already. In the condition of our prisoners (for so I will call them for shortness sake) you may see the student's paradox, *nunquam minus solus quam cum solus*, realized in a new way: to the keeper, a *multitude*, though not a *crowd*; to themselves, they are *solitary* and *sequestered individuals*.

What is more, you will see this purpose answered more completely by this plan, than it could possibly be on any other. What degree of solitude it was proposed to reduce them to in the once-intended penitentiary-houses, need not be considered. But for one purpose, in buildings of any mode of construction that could then and there have been in view, it would have been necessary, according to the express regulations of that plan, that the law of solitude should be dispensed with; I mean, so often as the prisoners were to receive the benefits of attendance on Divine service. But in my brother's circular penitentiary-houses, they might receive these benefits, in every circumstance, without stirring from their cells. No thronging nor jostling in the way between the scene of work and the scene destined to devotion; no quarrellings, nor confederatings, nor plottings to escape; nor yet any whips or fetters to prevent it.

Letter IX.: Penitentiary-houses—economy—contract—plan.

I am come now to the article of *pecuniary economy*; and as this is the great rock upon which the original penitentiary-plan I understand has split, I cannot resist the temptation of throwing out a few hints relative to the mode of management, which I look upon as the most eligible in this view; but which could not, as you will see, have been established with anything like the advantage, upon any other ground than that of my brother's inspection principle.

To come to the point at once, I would do the whole by *contract*. I would farm out the profits, the no-profits, or if you please the losses, to him who, being in other respects unexceptionable, offered the best terms. Undertaking an enterprise new in its extent, in the description of the persons to be subjected to his management, and in many other circumstances, his success in if, if he does succeed, may be regarded in the light of an invention, and rewarded accordingly, just as success in other inventions is rewarded, by the profit which a monopoly secured by patent enables a man to make; and that in proportion to the success which constitutes their merit. He should have it during *good behaviour*; which you know is as much as to say, unless specific instances of misbehaviour, flagrant enough to render his removal expedient, be proved on him in a legal way, he shall have it for his *life*. Besides that when thus secured he can afford to give the better price for his bargain, you will presently see more material reasons to counterbalance the seeming unthriftiness of granting him a term, which may prove so long a one. In other respects, the terms of the contract must, of course, depend upon the proportion of capital, of which the contract gave him the use. Supposing the advance to amount to the whole manufacturing stock, he must of course either pay something for his contract, or be contented with a share of the gross profits, instead of the whole, unless that from such profits an interest upon the capital so advanced to him should be deducted: in which case, nobody, I suppose, would grudge him the whole net profit after such deduction, even though the rate of interest were much below the ordinary one: the difference between such reduced rate of interest and the ordinary one, would constitute the whole of the expense which the public would be at. Suppose, to speak at random, this expense were to amount to £6000, £8000, or £10,000 a-year, for the 3000 convicts which, it was computed, would be the standing number to be maintained in England, I should not imagine that such a sum as even this latter would be much grudged. I fancy the intended expedition to Botany Bay, of which I am just apprized, will be rather more expensive. Not that it appears to me that the nation would remain saddled with any such expense as this at the long run, or indeed with any part of it. But of this hereafter.

In the next place, I would give my contractor all the *powers* that his interest could prompt him to wish for, in order to enable him to make the most of his bargain, with only some slight reservations, which I will mention afterwards; for very slight ones you will find they will be, that can be needful or even serviceable in the view of preventing abuse.

But the greater latitude he has in taking such measures, the less will he grudge the letting it be known what the measures are which he *does* take, knowing, at the same time, that no advantage can be taken of such knowledge, by turning him out in case of his success, and putting in another to reap the fruits of his contrivance. I will then require him to *disclose*, and even to print and *publish* his accounts— the whole process and detail of his management—the whole history of the prison. I will require him, I say, on pain of forfeiture or other adequate punishment, to publish these accounts, and that upon oath. I have no fear of his not publishing *some* accounts, because, if the time is elapsed and some accounts not published—a fact not liable to dispute—the punishment takes place of course: and I have not much fear that the accounts, when published, will not be *true*; because, having power to do every thing that is for his advantage, there is nothing which it is his interest to conceal; and the interest which the punishment for perjury gives him not to conceal, is manifest, more especially as I make him examinable and cross-examinable *viva voce* upon oath at any time.

It is for clearing away as much as possible every motive of pecuniary interest that could prompt him to throw any kind of cloak or reserve upon any of his expedients for increasing his profits, that I would insure them to him for *life*.

From the information thus got from him, I derive this advantage. In the case of his *ill* success, I see the causes of it, and not only I, but every body else that pleases, may see the causes of it; and amongst the rest, those who, in case of their taking the management out of his hands, would have an interest in being acquainted with such causes, in order to obviate or avoid them. More than that, if his ill success is owing to incapacity, and that incapacity such as, if continued, might raise my expense above the calculation, I can make him stop in time—a measure to which he can have as little objection as myself; for it is one advantage of this plan, that whatever mischief happens must have more than eaten out all *his* profits before it reaches *me*.

In the case of his good success, I see the causes of that too; and every body sees them, as before; and, amongst others, all persons who could propose to themselves to get into a situation similar to his, and who in such case would naturally promise themselves, in the event of their getting into his situation, a success equal to his—or rather superior; for such is the presumption and vanity natural to man.

Without such publication, whom should I have to deal with, besides him? certainly, in comparison, but a very few; not many more than I may have had at first: the terms, of course, disadvantageous as at first; for disadvantageous terms at first, while all is yet in darkness, they certainly must be.

After such publication, whom should I have then? I should have every body; every body who, by fortune, experience, judgment, disposition, should conceive himself able, and find himself inclined, to engage in such a business; and each person seeing what advantage had been made, and how, would be willing to make his offer in proportion. What situation more favourable for making the best terms?

These best terms, then, I should make at his death, even for his establishment; but long before that, had I others upon the carpet, I should make similar good terms for all those others. Thus I make his advantage mine, not only after it has ceased to be his, but almost as soon as it commences so to be: I thus get his success in all the rest, by paying for it only in the one; and in that not more than it was necessary to pay for it.

But *contractors*, you will say perhaps, or at least if you don't, there are enough that will, *"are a good-for-nothing set of people; and why should we be fleeced by them? One of them perjured himself not long ago, and we put him into the pillory. They are the same sort of gentry that are called farmers-general in France, and publicans in the Gospel, where they are ranked with sinners; and nobody likes them anywhere."* All this, to be sure, is very true: but if you put one of them into the pillory, you put another of them into the *post-office*; and if in the devoted city five righteous would have screened the whole gang from the perdition called for by the enormities of ninety-five unrighteous, why should not the merits of one Palmer be enough to make it up for the demerits of twenty Atkinsons? Gentlemen in general, as I have had manifold occasion to observe, love close reasoning, and here they have it. It might be thought straying from the point, if I ventured to add, that gentlemen in the corn trade, or in any other trade, have not commonly quite so many witnesses to *their bargains*, as my contractor would have to the management of *his* house.

Letter X.: Choice of Trades Should Be Free.

In my last I troubled you with my sentiments on the duration of the first contract, and the great article of *publicity* in the management, which was my motive for admitting of a duration so unlimited. But long before my contractor and I had come to any settlement about these points, he would have found various questions to propose to me. One thing he would not fail to say to me is—*What trades may I put my men to when I have got them?* My answer is soon given. *Any whatever that you can persuade them to turn their hands to.* Now, then, Sir, let us think for a moment, if you please, what trades it may be most for his *advantage* to put them to, and what it is therefore *most likely* he should be disposed to put them to.

That he may get the better view of them, I throw them into *four* classes. In the *first*, I place those who already are possessed of businesses capable of being carried on with advantage in the prison: in the *second*, those trained up to businesses which, though not capable in themselves of being carried on within such limits, yet by the similarity of operation have a tendency to render it more or less easy for a man to learn some of those other businesses which *are*: in the *third* rank, I would place such as had been trained up indeed to industry, but to branches which have no such tendency as I have just mentioned; such, for instance, as porters, coalheavers, gardeners, and husbandmen. In the last I would place men regularly brought up to the profession of thieving, and others who have never been brought up to any kind of industry. Some names for these different classes I may as well endeavour to find as not; for names they must have when they get into their house; and if I perform not that business myself, somebody else must do it for me. I will call them the *good* hands, the *capable* hands, the *promising* hands, and the *drones*. As to the *capable* hands, they will, of course, be the more valuable, the nearer the businesses they understand approach to those of the *good* ones; in other words, the less difficulty there would be in teaching the latter the business of the former. The same observation of course applies to the *promising* hands; in as far as the advantage which the one possess by habit the others may appear to possess by disposition. Lower down in the scale of detail I will not attempt to lead you.

You have a very pretty law in England for enriching the country, by keeping boys backward, and preventing men from following the trades they could get most by. If I were jealous of Russia's growing too rich, and being able to buy too many of our goods, I would try to get such a law as that introduced among these stupid people here, who have never yet had the sense to think of any such thing. Having no such jealousy against any country, much less against my own Utopia, I would beg that law might be banished from within my walls. I fancy my contractor would be as well pleased with its room as its company; and as the same indulgence has been granted to other persons of whose industry no great jealousy seems to be entertained, such as soldiers and sailors, I have no great fear the indulgence would be denied me. Much I believe is not apprehended in that way from the red-coats and jack-tars; and still less, I believe, would be apprehended from my heroes.

This stumbling-block cleared away, the first thing I imagine my contractor would do, would be to set to work his *good* hands; to whom he would add as many of his *capable* hands as he could muster.

With his *promising* hands and his drones, he would set up a manufacture. What, then, shall this manufacture be? *It may be this, and that, and t'other thing,* says the hard-labour bill: *it shall be anything or everything,* say I.

As to the question, *What sort of manufacture or manufacturer would be likely to answer best?* it is a discussion I will not attempt to lead you into, for I do not propose at present to entertain you with a critical examination of the several actual and possible manufactures, established and establishable in Great Britain. The case, I imagine, would be, that some manufacturer or other would be the man I should have for my contractor—a man who, being engaged in some sort of business that was easy to learn, and doing pretty well with as many hands as he was able to get upon the ordinary terms, might hope to do better still with a greater number, whom he could get upon much better terms. Now, whether there are any such manufacturers, and how many, is what I cannot so well tell you, especially at this distance; but, if you think it worth while to ask Mr. Daily Advertiser, or Mr. St. James' Chronicle, I fancy it will not be long before you get some answer.

In my *View of the Hard-Labour Bill*, I ventured to throw out a hint upon the subject of putting the good hands to their own trades. Whether any and what use was made of that hint, I cannot recollect; for neither the act which passed afterwards, nor any chapter of that history, has travelled with me to *Crecheff*; nor should I have had a single scrap of paper to refresh my memory on that subject, but for the copy of my own pamphlet which I found on my brother's shelf. The general notion seemed to be, that as the people were to be made to work for their punishment, the works to be given to them should be somewhat which they would not like; and, in that respect, it looks as if the consideration of punishment, with its appendage of reformation, had kept the other of economy a little behind the curtain. But I neither see the great danger nor the great harm of a man's liking his work too well; and how well soever he might have liked it *elsewhere*, I should still less apprehend his liking the thought of having it to do *there*. Supposing no sage regulations made by any body to nail them to this or that sort of work, the work they would naturally fall upon under the hands of a contractor would be that, whatever it might be, by which there was most money to be made; for the more the prisoner-workman got, the more the master could get out of him; so that upon that point I should have little fear of their not agreeing. Nor do I see why labour should be the less *reforming* for being profitable. On the contrary, among working men, especially among working men whom the discipline of the house would so effectually keep from all kinds of mischief, I must confess I know of no test of reformation so plain or so sure as the improved quantity and value of their work.

It looks, however, as if the authors of the above provision had not quite so much faith in such an arrangement as I must confess I have. For the choice of the trade was not to be left to the governor of the prison, much less to the prisoner-workman, but was given to *superintending committees of justices of the peace.* In choosing among the employments exemplified, and other similar ones (for if I mistake not this restriction of similarity was subjoined) it was indeed recommended to those magistrates to take "such employments as they should deem most conducive to profit." But the profit here declared to be in view was, not the profit of the *workman* or his master the *governor*, but I know not what profit "of the *district*," the "convenience" of which (though I know not what convenience there could be, distinct from profit) was another land-mark given them to steer by. If you cast an eye on the trades exemplified (as I believe I must beg you to do presently) you will find some difficulty, I believe, in conceiving that in the choice of them the article of profit could have been the uppermost consideration. Nor was this all; for besides the vesting of the choice of the employments in committees of justices in the first instance, the same magistrates are called upon to exercise their judgment and ingenuity in dividing the prisoners into classes; in such sort, that the longer a man had stayed in the house his labour should be less and less "severe," exception made for delinquency, in which case a man might at any time be turned down from an upper class to a lower. But had the matter been left to a contractor and his prisoner-workmen, they would have been pretty sure to pitch upon, and to stick to, what would be most conducive to *their* profit, and by *that* means to the profit of the district; and that without any recommendation. Whether the effect of that recommendation would have been equally sure upon the above-mentioned magistrates, would have remained to be decided by experience. Understanding me to be speaking merely of a magistrate in the abstract, you will forgive my saying, that in this one point I have not quite so great a confidence in a set of gentlemen of that description, as I have in that sort of knave called a contractor. I see no sort of danger, that to the contractor there should be any one object upon earth dearer than the interest of the contractor; but I see some danger that there may be, now and then by accident, some other object rather dearer to the magistrate. Among these rival objects, if we do not always reckon the pleasure of plaguing the contractor, should he and the magistrate chance not to agree, we may however not unfrequently reckon the exercise of his (the magistrate's) own power, and the display of his own wisdom; the former of which, he may naturally enough conceive, was not given to him for nothing, nor the latter confided in without cause. You must, I think, before now have met with examples of men, that had rather a plan of the public's, or even of an individual's for whom they had a more particular regard, should miscarry under their management, than prosper under a different one.

But if, without troubling yourself about general theories of human nature, you have a mind for a more palpable test of the propriety of this reasoning, you may cut the matter short enough, by making an experiment upon a contractor, and trying whether he will give you as good terms with these clogs about him, as he would without them. Sure I am, that, were I in his place, I should require no small abatement to be made to me, if, instead of choosing the employments for my own men, I was liable at every turn to have them taken out of my hands and put to different employments, by A, B, and C to-day, and by X, Y, and Z to-morrow.

Upon the whole, you will not wonder that I should have my doubts at present, whether the plan was rendered much better for these ingenious but complicated refinements. They seemed mighty fine to me at the time, for when I saw contrivance, I expected success proportionable.

Letter XI.: Multiplication of Trades Is Not Necessary.

So far as to the *choice* of businesses: As to the new ones, I see no reason why any point should be made of *multiplying* them: a single one, well chosen, may answer the purpose, just as well as ever so many more. I mention this, because though it may be easy to find one species of manufacture, or five, or ten, that might answer with workmen so cramped, and in a situation so confined, it might not be quite so easy to find fifty or a hundred. The number of hands for which employment is to be found, can scarcely be admitted as a reason for multiplying the subjects of manufacture. In such a nation as Great Britain, it is difficult to conceive that the greatest number of hands that can be comprised in such an establishment, should be great enough to overstock the market; and if this island of ours is not big enough, this globe of ours is still bigger. In many species of manufacture, the work is performed with more and more advantage, as every body knows, the more it can be divided; and, in many instances, what sets bounds to that division, is rather the number of hands the master can afford to maintain, than any other circumstance.

When one turns to the hard-labour bill, it looks as if the framers of it had been under some anxiety to find out businesses that they thought might do in their penitentiary-houses, and to make known the result of their discoveries. It accordingly proposes for consideration a variety of examples. For such of the prisoners as were to be worked the hardest: 1. treading in a wheel; 2. drawing in a capstern for turning a mill or other machine or engine; 3. beating hemp; 4. rasping logwood; 5. chopping rags; 6. sawing timber; 7. working at forges; 8. smelting. For those who are to be most favoured: 1. making ropes; 2. weaving sacks; 3. spinning yarn; 4. knitting nets.

I find some difficulty, however, in conceiving to what use this instruction was destined, unless it were the edification of that class of legislators, more frequently quoted for worth than knowledge— the country gentlemen. To some gentlemen of that respectable description, it might, for aught I know, be matter of consolation to see that industry could find so many shapes to assume, on such a stage. But if it was designed to give a general view of the purposes to which manual labour may be applied, it goes not very far, and there are publications enough that go some hundreds of times farther. If the former of its two chapters was designed as a specimen of such works of a particularly laborious cast, as are capable of being carried on to the greatest advantage, or with least advance of capital, or with the greatest security, against workmen of so refractory a complexion—or if either chapter was destined as a specimen of employments that required least extent of room—in any of these cases the specimen seems not a very happy one:—1st and 2d, Of the *treading in a wheel*, or *drawing in a capstern for turning a mill*, nothing can be said in respect of pecuniary productiveness, till the mill, the machine, or the engine, are specified; nor anything that can be found to distinguish them from other employments, except the room and the expense which such implements seem more particularly to require, 3d, *Beating of hemp* is a business too proverbial to be unknown to any body, and in those establishments where it has had compulsion for its motive, has not hitherto, I believe, proved a very profitable one; and if I may believe people who are of the trade, and who have no interest to mialead me, hemp beaten by hand, though it takes more labour, does not fetch so good a price, as when beaten at a water-mill. 4th, *Rasping logwood* is an employment which is said by Mr. Howard, I think, and others, to be carried on in some work-houses of Holland, and I believe to some profit. But I know it has been carried on likewise by the natural *primum mobiles*; witness a wind-mill, which, I remember, a tenant of yours employed in this way; and I can conceive few operations in which those natural powers promise to have greater advantage over the human. 5th, *Chopping rags* is a business that can answer no other purpose than the supplying materials for paper-mills, which cannot anywhere be established without a supply of *running-water*—an element which, I am sure in many, and, I am apt to think, in all paper-mills hitherto established, affords for this operation a *primum mobile* much more advantageous than human labour. In the 6th, 7th, and 8th examples, viz. *sawing timber, working at forges*, and *smelting,* I see nothing to distinguish them very remarkably from three hundred others that might be mentioned, unless it be the great room they all of them occupy, the great and expensive establishment which they suppose, or the dangerous weapons which they put into the hands of any workman who may be disposed to turn that property to account. *9th,* As to *rope making,* which stands at the head of the less laborious class, besides being, as I always understood, remarkably otherwise, it has the particular property of taking up more room than, I believe, any other manufacturing employment that was ever thought of. As to the three last articles of the dozen, viz. *weaving sacks, spinning yarn, and knitting nets,* I know of no particular objections that can be made to them, any more than to three score others. But, without going a stone's throw from the table I am writing upon, I could find more than as many businesses, which pay better in England, than these three last, in other respects exceptionable ones, which are as easy to learn, take up as little room, and require a capital nearly, or quite as moderate, to set up. By coming here, if I have learnt nothing else, I have learnt what the human powers are capable of, when unfettered by the arbitrary regulations of an unenlightened age; and gentlemen may say what they please, but they shall never persuade me that in England those powers are in any remarkable degree inferior to what they are in Russia. However, not having the mantle of legislation to screen me from the ridicule of going beyond my last, I forbear to specify even what I have under my eye, knowing that in Mr. Arthur Young, a gentleman whom no one can accuse of hiding his candle under a bushel, anybody that chooses it might find an informant, who, on this, as well as so many other important subjects, for every grain of information I could give, could give a thousand.

But without any disparagement to that gentleman, for whose public-spirited labours and well-directed talents no man feels greater respect than I do, there are other persons, who on these same subjects could, for such a purpose, give still more and better information than he, and who would not be less communicative: I mean, as before, Mr. Daily Advertiser and his brethren.

There are two points in politics very hard to compass. One is, to persuade legislators that they do not understand shoemaking better than shoemakers; the other is, to persuade shoemakers that they do not understand legislating better than legislators. The latter point is particularly difficult in our own dear country; but the other is the hardest of all hard things everywhere.

Letter XII.: Contractor's Checks.

The point, then, being settled, what trades the people may be employed in, another question my contractor will ask is, what powers he is to have put into his hands, as a means of persuading them to betake themselves to those trades? The shortest way of answering this question will be to tell him what powers he shall *not* have. In the first place then, he shall not starve them. "What then," you will say perhaps, "do you think it likely that he would?" To speak the truth, for my own part I have no great fear of it. But others perhaps might. Besides, my notion is, that the law, in guarding itself against men, ought to do just the contrary of what the judge should do in trying them, especially where there is nothing to be lost by it. The business, you know, of the judge, is to presume them all honest till he is forced to suspect the contrary: the business of the law is to conclude them all, without exception, to be the greatest knaves and villains that can be imagined. My contractor, therefore, I make myself sure, would starve them — a good many of them at least — if he were let alone. He would starve, of course, all whom he could not make pay for their board, together with something for his trouble. But as I should get nothing by this economy, and might lose some credit by it, I have no mind it should take place. Bread, though as bad as wholesome bread can be, they shall have, then, in plenty: this and water, and nothing else. This they shall be certain of having, and, what is of full as much consequence, every body else that pleases shall be certain of their having it. My brethren of the would-be-reforming tribe may go and look at it at the baker's: they may weigh it, if they will, and buy it, and carry it home, and give it to their children or their pigs. It shall be dealt out by sound of trumpet, if you please; and Christian starers may amuse themselves with seeing bad bread dealt out to felons, as Christian ambassadors are entertained with the sight of bags of bad money counted out to Janissaries. The latter wonder I saw: the other I assure you would give me much more pleasure.

With this saving clause, I deliver them over to the extortioner, and let him make the most of them. Let him sell porter at the price of port:

and "humble port" at the price of "imperial tokay:" his customers might grumble, but I don't think you would, and I am sure I should not: for it is for that they were put there. Never fear his being so much his own enemy, as to stand out for a price which nobody will give.

In the next place I don't know that I should be for allowing him the power of beating his boarders, nor, in short, of punishing them in any shape. Anywhere else, such an exemption must have been visionary and impracticable. Without either punishment, or interest given him in the profits of his labour—an interest which, to get the better of so many adverse motives, must have been a pretty strong one, how could you have insured a man's doing a single stroke of work? and, even with such interest, how could you have insured his not doing all sorts of mischief? As to mischief, I observed to you, under the article of safe custody, how easy their keeper might make himself upon that score: and as to work, I flatter myself you perceive already, that there need be no great fear of a want of inducements adequate to that purpose.

If, after all, it should be insisted that some power of correction would be absolutely necessary—for instance, in the case of a prisoner's assaulting a keeper or teacher at the time of receiving his food or his instruction (a case which, though never very probable, would be always possible)—such a power, though less necessary here than anywhere else, might, on the other hand, be given with less danger. What tyranny could subsist under such a perfect facility of complaint as is the result of so perfect a facility of inspection? But on this head a word is sufficient, after what I have said in considering the general heads of advantage dependent on this principle. Other checks assistant to this are obvious enough. A *correction-book* might be kept, in which every instance of chastisement, with the cause for which it was administered, might be entered upon record: any the slightest act of punishment not entered to be considered as a lawless injury. If these checks be not enough, the presence of one or more persons, besides him by whom the correction was actually administered. might be required as witnesses of the mode and quantum of correction, and of the alleged cause.

But, besides preventing his starving them or using them ill, there is another thing I should be much inclined to do, in order to make it his interest to take care of them. I would make him pay so much for every one that died, without troubling myself whether any care of his could have kept the man alive. To be sure, he would make me pay for this in the contract; but as I should receive it from him afterwards, what it cost me in the long run would be no great matter. He would get underwriter's profit by me; but let him get that, and welcome.

Suppose three hundred prisoners; and that, out of that number of persons of their ages, ten, that is, one out of thirty, ought to die every year, were they taken at large. But persons of their character and in their condition, it may be expected, will die faster than honest men. Say, therefore, one in twenty, though I believe, as jails stand at present, if no more than one in ten die, or, for aught I know. out of a much smaller number, it may be thought very well. Give the contractor, then, for every man that ought to die, for instance ten pounds: that sum, repeated for every man in twenty among three hundred, will amount to a hundred and fifty pounds. Upon these terms, then, at the end of the year make him pay ten pounds for every man that has actually died within that time; to which you may add, *or escaped*, and I dare say he will have no objection. If by nursing them and making much of them he should find himself at the end of the year a few pounds the richer by his tenderness, who would grudge it him? If you have still any doubt of him, instead of the ten pounds you may put twenty: you will not be much the poorer for it. I don't know, upon second thoughts, whether somewhat of this sort has not been put in practice, or at least proposed, for foundlings. Be that as it may, make but my contractor's allowance large enough, and you need not doubt of his fondness of these his adopted children; of whom whosoever may chance while under his wing to depart this vale of tears, will be sure to leave one sincere mourner at least, without the parade of mourning.

Some perhaps may be for observing, that, upon my own principles, this contrivance would be of no use but to save the useless, since the contractor, of himself, knows better things than not to take care of a cow that will give milk. But, with their leave, I do not mean that even the useless should be starved; for if the judges had thought this proper, they would have said so.

The patrons of the hard-labour bill, proceeding with that caution and tenderness that pervades their whole system, have denied their *governor*, as they call him, the power of whipping. Some penal power, however, for putting a stop to mischief, was, under their plan, absolutely necessary. They preferred, as the mildest and less dangerous power, that of confining a man in a *dark dungeon under ground*, under a bread-and-water diet. I did then take the liberty to object against the choosing, by way of punishment, the putting of a man into a place which differed not from other places in any essential particular, but that of the chance it stood of proving unwholesome; proposing, at the same time, a very simple expedient, by which their ordinary habitations might be made to receive every other property of a dungeon; in short, the making of them dark.

But in one of my brother's inspection-houses, there the man is in his dungeon already (the only sort of dungeon, at least, which I conceive any man need be in,) very safe and quiet. He is likewise entertaining himself with his bread and water, with only one little circumstance in his favour, that whenever he is tired of that regimen, it is in his own power to put himself under a better: unless my contractor chooses to fine himself for the purpose of punishing his boarder—an act of cruelty which I am in no great dread of.

In short, bating the checks you have seen, and which certainly are not very complicated, the plan of establishment which such a principle of construction seems, now at least, if not for the first time, to render eligible, and which as such I have been venturing to recommend, is exactly upon a par, in point of simplicity, with the forced and temporary expedient of the *ballast-lighters*—a plan that has the most perfect simplicity to recommend it, and, I believe, not much else. The chief differences are, that convicts are not, in the inspection-houses, as in those lighters, jammed together in fetters under a master subject to no inspection, and scarce under any

controul, having no interest in their welfare or their work, in a place of secret confinement, favourable to infection and to escapes.

Letter XIII.: Means of Extracting Labour.

Understanding thus much of his situation, my contractor, I conceive, notwithstanding the checks you have seen, will hardly think it necessary to ask me how he is to manage to persuade his boarders to set to work.—Having them under this regimen, what better security he can wish for of their working, and that to their utmost, I can hardly imagine. At any rate, he has much better security than he can have for the industry and diligence of any ordinary journeyman at large, who is paid by the day, and not by the piece. If a man won't work, nothing has he to do, from morning to night, but to eat his bad bread and drink his water, without a soul to speak to. If he will work, his time is occupied, and he has his meat and his beer, or whatever else his earnings may afford him, and not a stroke does he strike but he gets something, which he would not have got otherwise. This encouragement is necessary to his doing his utmost: but more than this is not necessary. It is necessary every exertion he makes should be sure of its reward; but it is not necessary that such reward be so great, or any thing near so great, as he might have had, had he worked elsewhere. The confinement, which is his punishment, preventing his carrying the work to another market, subjects him to a monopoly; which the contractor, his master, like any other monopolist, makes, of course, as much of as he can. The workman lives in a poor country, where wages are low; but in a poor country, a man who is paid according to his work will exert himself at least as much as in a rich one. According to Mr. Arthur Young, and the very cogent evidence he gives, he should work more: for more work that intelligent traveller finds always done in dear years than in plentiful ones: the earnings of one day affording, in the latter case, a fund for the extravagance of the next. But this is not all. His master may fleece him, if he pleases, at both ends. After sharing in his profits, he may again take a profit upon his expense. He would probably choose to employ both expedients together. The tax upon earnings, if it stood alone, might possibly appear liable to be evaded in some degree, and be frustrated in some cases, by a confederacy between the workmen and their employers out of doors; the tax upon expenditure, by their frugality, supposing that virtue to take root in such a soil; or in some instances, perhaps, by their generosity to their friends without doors. The tax upon earnings would probably not be laid on in an open way, upon any other than the *good* hands; whose traffic must be carried on, with or without his intervention, between them and their out-of-door employers. In the trades which he thought proper to set up of himself for his *capable* hands, his *promising* hands, and his *drones*, the tax might be levied in a more covert way by the lowering of the price paid by him, in comparison of the free prices given out of doors for similar work. Where he is sure of his men, as well with regard to their disposition to spend as with regard to their inability to collude, the tax upon expenditure, without any tax upon profits open or covert, would be the least discouraging: it would be the least discouraging for the present, as the earnings would sound greater to their ears; and with a view to the future, as they would thereby see (I mean such of them as had any hopes of releasement) what their earnings might at that happy period be expected to amount to, in reality as well as in name.

Letter XIV.: Provision For Liberated Persons.

The circumstance touched upon at the close of my last letter, suggests another advantage, and that not an inconsiderable one, which you will find more particularly, if not exclusively, connected with the contract plan.

The turning of the prisoners' labour into the most profitable channels being left free, depending upon the joint choice of the two only parties interested in pushing the advantage to the utmost, would afford a resource, and that I should conceive a sure one, for the subsistence of the prisoners, after the expiration of their terms. No trade that could be carried on in this state of thraldom, but could be carried on with at least equal advantage in a state of liberty. Both parties would probably find their account in continuing their manufacturing connexion, after the dissolution of every other. The workman, after the stigma cast on him by the place of his abode, would probably not find it so easy to get employment elsewhere. If he got it at all, it would be upon terms proportioned in some measure to the risk which an employer at large might think he would run on his own part, and in some cases to the danger of driving away fellow-workmen, by the introduction of an associate who might prove more or less unwelcome. He would therefore probably come cheaper to his former master than another man would; at the same time that he would get more from him in his free state than he had been used to get when confined.

Whether this resource was in contemplation with the planners of the hard-labour bill, I cannot pretend to say: I find not upon the face of that bill any proof of the affirmative. It provides a sum for each prisoner, partly for present subsistence, partly as a sort of little capital to be put into his pocket upon his discharge. But the sole measure assigned to this sum is the good behaviour of the party, not the sum required to set him up in whatever might have been his trade. Nor had the choice of his employment been left to the governor of the house, still less to the prisoner, but to committees of justices, as I observed before.

As to the Woolwich Academy, all ideas of reformation under that name, and of a continuance of the like industry as a means of future provision, seem there to have been equally out of the question. That they should hire lighters of their own to heave ballast from, does not appear to have been expected; and if any of them had had the fortune to possess trades of their own before, the scraping of gravel for three, five, or seven years together out of the river, had no particular tendency, that I can see, to rub up the recollection of those trades. The allowance upon discharge would, however, always have its use, though not always the same use. It might help to fit them out for trades; it might serve them to get drunk with; it might serve them to buy any house-breaking implements which they could not so well come at to steal.—The separation between the landlord and his guests must on his side have been rendered the less affecting, by the expectation which he could not but entertain of its proving but a short one. Nor was subsequent provision of one sort or other by any means wanting, for those who failed to find it *there*. The gallows was always ready with open arms to receive as many as the jail-fever should have refused.

Letter XV.: Prospect of Saving From This Plan.

Many are the data with which a man ought to be furnished (and with not one of which am I furnished) before he pretended to speak upon any tolerable footing of assurance with regard to the advantage that might be expected in the view of pecuniary economy from the inspection plan. *On the one hand,* the average annual amount of the *present* establishments, whatever they are (for I confess I do not know,) for the disposal of convicts: The expected amount of the like average with regard to the measure which I have just learnt has been resolved upon, for sending colonies of them to New South Wales, including as well the maintenance of them till shipped, as the expense of the transportation, and the maintenance of them when they are got there:—*On the other hand,* the capital proposed to have been expended in the *building* and *fitting up* the experimental *penitentiary house:*—The further capital proposed to have been expended in the *furniture* of it:—The sum proposed to have been allowed per man for the *maintenance* of the prisoners till the time when their labour might be expected to yield a produce. These points and a few others being ascertained, I should then be curious to know what degree of productiveness, if any, would be looked upon as giving to the measure of a penitentiary-house, either of any construction or of this extraordinary one, the pre-eminence upon the whole over any of the other modes of disposal now in practice or in contemplation. Many distinct points for the eye to rest upon in such a scale will readily occur:—*1st,* The produce might be barely sufficient to pay the expense of *feeding;*—*2d,* It might farther pay the expense of *clothing;*—*3d,* It might farther pay the expense of *guarding* and *instructing,* viz. the salaries or other emoluments of the numerous tribe of visitors, governors, jailors, task-masters, &c. in the one case, and of the contractor and his assistants in the other;—*4th,* It might farther pay the *wear and tear* of the working-stock laid in;—*5th,* It might farther pay the *interest* of the *capital* employed in the purchase of such stock;—*6th,* It might farther pay the interest of the capital laid out in the *erecting* and *fitting* up the establishment in all its parts, at the common rate of interest for money laid out in building;—*7th,* It might farther pay, at the ordinary rate, the *interest* of the money, if any, laid out in the *purchase* of the *ground*. Even at the first mentioned and lowest of these stages, I should be curious to compare the charge of such an institution with that of the least chargeable of those others that are as yet preferred to it. When it had arisen above the last, then, as you see, and not till then, it could be said to yield a profit, in the sense in which the same thing could be said of any manufacturing establishment of a private nature.

But long before that period, the objections of those whose sentiments are the least favourable to such an establishment would, I take for granted, have been perfectly removed. Yet what should make it stop anywhere short of the highest of those stages, or what should prevent it from rising even considerably above the highest of them, is more, I protest, than I can perceive. In what points a manufacturer setting up in such an establishment would be in a *worse* situation than an ordinary manufacturer, I really do not see; but I see many points in which he is in a *better*. His hands, indeed, are all raw, perhaps, at least with relation to the particular species of work which he employs them upon, if not with relation to every other. But so are all hands everywhere, at the first setting up of every manufacture. Look round, and you will find instances enough of manufactures where children, down to four years old, earn something, and where children a few years older earn a subsistence, and that a comfortable one. I must leave to you to mention names and places. You, who have been so much of an English traveller, cannot but have met with instances in plenty, if you have happened to note them down. Many are the instances you must have found in which the part taken by each workman is reduced to some one single operation of such perfect simplicity, that one might defy the awkwardest and most helpless idler that ever existed to avoid succeeding in it. Among the eighteen or twenty operations into which the process of pin-making has been divided, I question whether there is any one that is not reduced to such a state. In this point, then, he is upon at least as good a footing as other manufacturers: but in all other points he is upon a better. What hold can any other manufacturer have upon his workmen, equal to what my manufacturer would have upon his? What other master is there that can reduce his workmen, if idle, to a situation next to starving, without suffering them to go elsewhere?

What other master is there, whose men can never get drunk unless he chooses they should do so? and who, so far from being able to raise their wages by combination, are obliged to take whatever pittance he thinks it most for his interest to allow? In all other manufactories, those members of a family who can and will work, must earn enough to maintain not only themselves but those who either cannot or will not work. Each master of a family must earn enough to maintain, or at least help to maintain a wife, and to maintain such as are yet helpless among his children. My manufacturer's workmen, however cramped in other respects, have the good or ill fortune to be freed from this incumbrance—a freedom, the advantage of which will be no secret to their master, who, seeing he is to have the honour of their custom in his capacity of shopkeeper, has taken care to get the measure of their earnings to a hair's-breadth. What other manufacturers are there who reap their profits at the risk of other people, and who have the purse of the nation to support them, in case of any blameless misfortune? And to crown the whole by the great advantage which is the peculiar fruit of this new principle, what other master or manufacturer is there, who to appearance constantly, and in reality as much as he thinks proper, has every look and motion of each workman under his eye? Without any of these advantages, we see manufacturers not only keeping their heads above water, but making their fortunes every day. A manufacturer in this situation *may* certainly fail, because so may he in any other. But the probability is, he would *not* fail: because, even without these great advantages, much fewer fail than thrive, or the wealth of the country could not have gone on increasing as it has done, from the reign of Brutus to the present. And if political establishments were to wait till probability were converted into certainty before trial, *Parliament* might as well go to bed at once, and sleep on the same pillow with sister *convocation.*

To speak in sober sadness, I do dearly love, as you well know, in human dealings no less than in divine, to think and to say, as far as conscience will allow me, that whatever is, is right;" as well concerning those things which are done, as concerning those which have been left undone. The gentlemen who gave themselves so much trouble about the penitentiary-house plan, did extremely well; and, for aught I know, the gentlemen who put it under the table at last, may have done still better. If you have a mind to share with me in this comfortable feeling, turn once more to that discarded favourite, and observe what load of expense, some part then necessary, some perhaps not altogether so, it was to have thrown upon the nation; and, at the same time, what will be still more comfortable to you, how great a proportion of that expense would be struck off, by the new and of course still greater favourite, which I have ventured to introduce to you.

In the first place, there was to have been a vast extent of ground; for it was to have had *rope-walks* and *timber-yards,* and it is well it was not to have had dock-yards. Then, for the sake of healthiness, that ground was to have a command of *running water:* then again, for the convenience of dignified inspectors, that ground and that water were to have been in the *vicinity of the metropolis.* It was to have been on the banks of the Thames—somewhere, I think, about Wandsworth and Battersea; and a site fit for I know not how many of the most luxurious villas that fancy could conceive or Christie describe, was to be buried under it. Seven-and-twenty thousand pounds, I think, was the price talked of, and, for aught I know, paid, for the bare ground, before so much as a spade was put in it. As to my contractor, eighteen or twenty acres of the most unprofitable land your country or any other contains, any waste land, in short, which the crown has already in its possession, would answer every plea he could put in; and out of that he would crib gardens for his own accommodation, and farm-yards, and I know not what besides. As to *running water,* it is indeed to every purpose a very agreeable circumstance, and, under the ordinary jail regimen, a very desirable, possibly an essential one. But many of the Lords and Commons make shift without it, even at their villas, and almost all of them when not at their villas, without ascribing any want of health they may labour under to the want of running water. As to my contractor's boarders, they must have water, indeed, because everybody must have water; but under the provision I have made for turning the operations of cleanliness into *motions of course,* I should apprehend their condition might still be tolerable, should they have no other running stock of that necessary element than what falls to the share of better men.

When the ground thus dearly wrung from the grasp of luxury came to be covered, think what another source of expense was to be opened, when, over and above nine hundred roomy chambers for so many persons to *lie* in, three other different classes of apartments were to be provided, to I know not what number nor extent, for them to *work* in, to *pray* in, and to *suffer* in! — four operations, the scenes of which are, upon our plan, consolidated into one.

I need not add much to what I have said in a former letter, about the tribe of subordinate establishments, each of them singly an object of no mean expense, which it seems to have been in contemplation to inclose within the fortress: I mean the mills, the forges, the engines, the timber-yards, and the rope-walks. The seal which stamps my contract dispels, as if it were a talisman, this great town in *nubibus;* and two or three plain round houses take its place. Either I am much mistaken, or a sum not much exceeding what was paid or destined for the bare ground of the proposed penitentiary-houses, would build and completely fit up those round houses, besides paying for the ground.

To this account of the *dead* stock is to be added, if I may say it without offence, that of the *live* stock of inspectors, of every rank and denomination: I mean the pyramid of under-keepers, and task-masters, and store-keepers, and governors, and committees of magistrates, which it builds up, all to be paid up and salaried, with allowances rising in proportion to the rise of dignity: the whole to be crowned with a grand triumvirate of superintendents, two of whom were to have been members of parliament, men of high birth and quality, whose toilsome dignity a minister would hardly have affronted by the offer of salaries much inferior to what are to be found annexed to sinecures.

I will not say much of the "other officers," without number, which I see, by my *View of the Hard-labour Bill*, were to have been added, and of course must have been added, in such number as the "committees" of your * * * * to whom this business was then committed, or at any rate some other good judges should have judged "necessary."

Officers and governors, *eo nomine,* my contractor would have none: and any superfluous clerk or over-looker, who might be found lurking in his establishment, he would have much less tenderness for, than your gardener has for the sow-thistles in your garden. The greatest part of *his* science comes to *him* in maxims from his grand-mother; and amongst the foremost of those maxims is that which stigmatizes as an unfrugal practice, the keeping of more cats than will catch mice.

If, under all these circumstances, the penitentiary-houses should have been somewhat of a bugbear, it will be the less to be wondered at, when one considers the magnitude of the scale upon which this complicated experiment was going to be made. I mentioned in round numbers nine hundred as the number of convicts which was going to be provided for; but 888 was the exact number mentioned in the bill. Three eights, "thus arranged, a terrible show!" But granting this to be the number likely to require provision of some kind or other, it surely does not follow that all that require it must necessarily be provided for in this manner, or in none. If the eight hundred and eighty eight appear so formidable, gentlemen may strike off the hundreds, and try whether the country will be ruined by an establishment inferior to that which an obscure ex-countryman of theirs is going to amuse himself with.

What I have all along been taking for granted is, that it is the mere dread of extravagance that has *driven* your thrifty minister from the penitentiary-house plan—not the love of transportation that has *seduced* him from it. The inferiority of the latter mode of punishment in point of exemplarity and equality—in short, in every point but that of expense, stands, I believe, undisputed. I collected the reasons against it, that were in every body's mouth, and marked them down, with, I think, some additions (as you may or may not remember) in my view of the hard-labour bill, supplement included. I have never happened to hear any objections made to those reasons; nor have I heard of any charms, other than those of antiquity and comparative frugality, that transportation has to recommend it. Supposing, therefore, what I most certainly do not suppose, that my contractor could not keep his people at home at *less* expense than it would take to send them abroad, yet if he could keep them at no *greater* expense, I should presume that even this would be reckoned no small point gained, and that even this very moderate success would be sufficient to put an end to so undesirable a branch of navigation.

Nor does any preference that might be given to the transportation plan, supersede the necessity of this or some other substitute to it, in the many cases to which it cannot be conceived that plan should be extended. Transportation to this desert for seven years—a punishment which under such circumstances is so much like transportation for life—is not, I suppose, to be inflicted for every peccadillo. Vessels will not be sailing every week or fortnight upon this four or five or six months navigation: hardly much oftener, I should suppose, than once a twelvemonth. In the meantime, the convicts must be somewhere: and whether they are likely to be better qualified for colonization by lounging in an ordinary jail, or rotting on board a ballast bulk, or working in an inspection-house, may now, I think, be left for any one to judge.

Letter XVI.: Houses of Correction.

In considering my brother's inspection plan as applicable to the purpose of establishments designed to force labour, my principal theme has hitherto been the national establishment of *penitentiary-houses*. My first design, however, was to help to drive the nail I saw agoing: I mean the *house of correction*, which the advertisement informed me was under consideration for your * * * *. I had little notion, at the outset, of attempting any such up-hill work as the heaving up again that huge stone, the *penitentiary-house*, which the builders at last had refused, and which, after the toiling and straining of so many years, had tumbled to the bottom. But the greater object grew upon me as I wrote; and what I found to say on that subject I grudged the less, as thinking it might, most of it, be more or less applicable to your establishment. How far, and in what particular respects, it may prove so, I have no means of knowing: I trouble you with it at a venture. In my last I proposed, if the nation were poor and fearful, a penitentiary-house upon a very small scale—so small, if such caution were thought necessary, as not to contain so many as a hundred prisoners. But however poor the nation may be, the * * * * * of * * * * surely is rich. What then should hinder your * * * * * from standing forth and setting the nation an example? What the number of persons you may have to provide for in this way is supposed to be, I have no means of knowing; but I should think it strange if it did not considerably exceed the one just mentioned. What it is you will risk by such an experiment, is more than I can see. As far as the building is concerned, it is a question which architects, and they alone, can answer. In the meantime, we who know nothing of the matter, can find no reason, all things considered, why a building upon this plan should cost more than upon another. But setting aside the building, every other difference is on the profitable side.

The precautions against escapes, and the restraints destined to answer the ends of punishment, would not, I suppose, in your establishment be quite so strict, as it would be necessary they should be in an establishment designed to answer the purpose of a penitentiary-house. Bars, bolts, and gratings, would in this of your's, I suppose, be rejected; and the inexorable *partition walls* might for some purposes be thinned away to boards or canvass, and for others thrown out altogether. With you, the gloomy paradox of crowded solitude might be exchanged, perhaps, for the cheerfulness of a common refectory. The Sabbath might be a Sabbath there as elsewhere. In the penitentiary inspection-house, the prisoners were to lie, as they were to eat, to work, to pray, and to do every thing, in their cells, and nowhere else. In your house of correction, where they should lie, or how they should lie, I stay not to inquire.

It is well, however, for you * * * * gentlemen, that you are so rich; for in point of frugality, I could not venture to promise you anything like the success that I would to "poor old England." Your contractor's jailbirds, if you had a contractor, would be perpetually upon the wing: the short terms you would be sending them to him for, would seldom admit of their attaining to such a proficiency, as to make a profit upon any branch of industry. In general, what in a former letter I termed the *good* hands, would be his chief, if not his whole dependence; and that, I doubt, but a scanty one.

I will not pester you with further niceties applicable to the difference between *houses of correction,* and *work-houses,* and *poor-houses,* if any there should be, which are not work-houses; between the different modes of treatment that may be due to what are looked upon as the inferior degrees of *dishonesty,* to *idleness* as yet untainted with dishonesty, and to blameless *indigence.* The law herself has scarcely eyes for these microscopic differences. I bow down, therefore, for the present at least, to the counsel of so many sages, and shrink from the crime of being "wiser than the law."

Letter XVII.: Prisons For Safe Custody Merely.

A word or two respecting the condition of *offenders before conviction:* or, if that expression should appear to include a solecism, of persons accused, who either for want of bail, or as charged with offences not bailable, have hitherto been made, through negligence or necessity, to share by anticipation so much of the fate of convicts, as imprisonment more or less rigid may amount to.

To persons thus circumstanced, the inspection principle would apply, as far as *safe custody* was concerned, with as much advantage as to convicts. But as there can be no ground for punishing them any otherwise than in so far as the *restraint* necessary for safe custody has the effect of punishment, there can be as little ground for subjecting them to *solitude;* unless where that circumstance should also appear necessary, either to safe custody, or to prevent that mental infection, which novices in the arts of dishonesty, and in debauchery, the parent of dishonesty, are so much in danger of contracting from the masters of those arts. In this view, therefore, the *partitions* might appear to some an unnecessary ingredient in the composition of the building; though I confess, from the consideration just alleged, they would not appear in that light to me. Communication must likewise be allowed to the prisoners with their friends and legal assistants, for the purpose of settling their affairs, and concerting their defence.

As forced labour is punishment, labour must not here be forced. For the same reason, and because the privation of such comforts of any kind as a man's circumstances allow him, is also punishment, neither should the free admission of such comforts, as far as is consistent with sobriety, be denied; nor, if the keeper is permitted to concern himself in any part of the trade, should he be permitted to make a greater profit than would be made by other traders.

But amongst persons of such description, and in such a multitude, there will always be a certain number, nor that probably an inconsiderable one, who will possess no means of subsistence whatever of their own. These then will, in so far, come under a predicament not very dissimilar to that of convicts in a penitentiary-house. Whatever works they may be capable of, there is no reason why subsistence should be given to them, any more than to persons free from suspicion and at large, but as the price for work, supposing them able to perform it. But as this ability is a fact, the judgment of which is a matter of great nicety, too much it may be thought by far to be entrusted to such hands, if to any, some allowance must therefore be made them *gratis*, and that at least as good a one as I recommended for the penitentiary-house. In order to supply the defects of this allowance, the point then will be, to provide some sort of work for such, who not having trades of their own which they can work at, are yet willing to take work, if they can get it. If to find such work might be difficult, even in a house of correction, on account of the shortness of the time which there may be for learning work, for the same reason it should be still more difficult in a prison appropriated to safe custody before conviction, at least in cases where, as it will sometimes happen, the commitment precedes the trial but a few days. If on the ground of being particularly likely to have it in his power to provide work, the contracting keeper of a penitentiary-house should be deemed the fittest person for the keeping of a *safe-custody house* (for so I would wish to call it, rather than a prison,) in other respects he might be thought less fit, rather than more so. In a penitentiary-house, he is an extortioner by trade: a trade he must wholly learn, every time he sets his foot in a safe-custody house, on pain of such punishment as unlicensed extortioners may deserve. But it by no means follows, because the keeper of a penitentiary-house has found one, or perhaps half-a-dozen sorts of work, any of which a person may make himself tolerably master of in the course of a few months, that he should be in possession of any that might be performed without learning, or learnt in a few days. If, therefore, for frugality's sake, or any other convenience, any other establishments were taken to combine with that of a safe-custody house, a house of correction would seem better suited to such a purpose, than a penitentiary-house. But without considering it as matter of necessity to have recourse to such shifts, the eligibility of which might depend upon local and other particular considerations, I should hope that employments would not be wanting, and those capable of affording a moderately good subsistence, for which a man of ordinary faculties would be as well qualified the first instant, as at the end of seven years. I could almost venture to mention examples, but that the reasons so often given stop my pen.

Letter XVIII.: Manufactories.

After so much as has been said on the application of our principle to the business of manufactories, considered as carried on by forced labour, you will think a very few words more than sufficient, in the view of applying it to manufactories carried on upon the ordinary plan of freedom.

The centrality of the presiding person's situation will have its use at all events; for the purpose of direction and order at least, if for no other. The concealment of his person will be of use, in as far as controul may be judged useful. As to partitions, whether they would be more serviceable in the way of preventing distraction, or disserviceable by impeding communication, will depend upon the particular nature of the particular manufacture. In some manufactories they will have a further use, by the convenience they may afford for ranging a greater number of tools than could otherwise be stowed within the workman's reach. In nice businesses, such as that of watch-making, where considerable damage might result from an accidental jog or a momentary distraction, such partitions, I understand, are usual.

Whatever be the manufacture, the utility of the principle is obvious and incontestible, in all cases where the workmen are paid according to their *time*. Where they are paid by the *piece,* there the interest which the workman has in the value of his work supersedes the use of coercion, and of every expedient calculated to give force to it. In this case, I see no other use to be made of the inspection principle, than in as far as instruction may be wanted, or in the view of preventing any waste or other damage, which would not of itself come home to the workman, in the way of diminishing his earnings, or in any other shape.

Were a manufactory of any kind to be established upon this principle, the *central lodge* would probably be made use of as the compting-house: and if more branches than one were carried on under the same roof, the accounts belonging to each branch would be kept in the corresponding parts of the lodge. The lodge would also serve as a sort of temporary store-room, into which the tools and materials would be brought from the work-houses, and from whence they would be delivered out to the workmen all around, as well as finished work received, as occasion might require.

Letter XIX.: Mad-houses.

I come now with pleasure, notwithstanding the sadness of the subject, to an instance in which the application of the principle will be of the lenient cast altogether: I mean, that of the melancholy abodes appropriated to the reception of the insane. And here, perhaps, a noble lord now in administration might find some little assistance lent to the humane and salutary regulations for which we are chiefly indebted to his care.

That any of the receptacles at present subsisting should be pulled down only to make room for others on the inspection principle, is neither to be expected nor to be wished. But, should any buildings that may be erected in future for this purpose be made to receive the inspection form, the object of such institutions could scarce fail of receiving some share of its salutary influence. The powers of the insane, as well as those of the wicked, are capable of being directed either against their fellow-creatures or against themselves. If in the latter case nothing less than perpetual chains should be availing, yet in all instances where only the former danger is to be apprehended, separate cells, exposed, as in the case of prisons, to inspection, would render the use of chains and other modes of corporal sufferance as unnecessary in this case as in any. And with regard to the conduct of the keepers, and the need which the patients have to be kept, the natural, and not discommendable jealousy of abuse would, in this instance as in the former ones, find a much readier satisfaction than it could anywhere at present.

But without thinking of erecting mad-houses on purpose, if we ask Mr. Howard, he will tell us, if I do not misrecollect, that there are few prisons or work-houses but what are applied occasionally to this use. Indeed, a receptacle of one or other of these descriptions is the ready, and, I believe, the only resource, which magistrates find vested in their hands. Hence it was, he so often found his senses assailed with that strange and unseemly mixture of calamity and guilt—lunatics raving and felons rioting in the same room. But in every penal inspection-house, every vacant cell would afford these afflicted beings an apartment exempt from disturbance, and adapted to their wants.

Letter XX.: Hospitals.

If any thing could still be wanting to show how far this plan is from any necessary connexion with severe and coercive measures, there cannot be a stronger consideration than that of the advantage with which it applies to *hospitals;* establishments of which the sole object is the relief of the afflicted, whom their own entreaties have introduced. Tenacious as ever of the principle of *omnipresence,* I take it for granted that the whole tribe of medical curators—the *surgeon,* the *apothecary,* the *matron,* to whom I could wish to add even the *physician,* could the establishment be but sufficient to make it worth his while, find in the inspection-lodge and what apartments might be added above it, their constant residence. Here the physician and the apothecary might know with certainty that the prescription which the one had ordered and the other made up, had been administered at the exact time and in the exact manner in which it was ordered to be administered. Here the surgeon would be sure that his instructions and directions had been followed in all points by his pupils and assistants. Here the faculty, in all its branches, might with the least trouble possible watch as much as they chose to watch, of the progress of the disease, and the influence of the remedy. Complaints from the sick might be received the instant the cause of the complaint, real or imaginary, occurred; though, as misconduct would be followed by instant reprehension, such complaints must be proportionably rare.

The separation of the cells might be in part, continued either for comfort or for decency. Curtains, instead of grating, would give the patients, when they thought fit, the option of being seen. Partitions of greater solidity and extent might divide the fabric into different wards, confining infection, adapting themselves to the varieties of disease. and affording, upon occasion, diversities of temperature.

In hot weather, to save the room from being heated, and the patients from being incommoded by the sun, *shades* or awnings might secure the windows towards the south.

I do not mean to entertain you here with a system of physic, or a treatise upon *airs*. But a word or two on this subject you must permit me. Would the ceilings of the cell be high enough? Is the plan of construction sufficiently favourable to ventilation? I have not the good fortune to have read a book published not long ago on the subject of hospitals, by our countryman Mr. Aikin, though I remember seeing some account of it in a review. But I cannot help begging of you to recommend to the notice of your medical friends, the perusal of Dr. De Maret's paper, in the *Memoirs of the Academy of Dijon* for the year 1782. If either his facts or his reasoning are to be trusted, not only no loftiness of ceiling is sufficient to ensure to such a building a purity of air, but it may appear questionable whether such an effect be upon the whole promoted by that circumstance.

His great anxiety seems to be, that at some known period or periods of the day, the whole mass of air may undergo at once a total change, not trusting to partial and precarious evacuations by opening here and there a window; still less to any height or other amplitude of room—a circumstance which of itself tends to render them still more partial and precarious. Proscribing all rectilinear walls and flat ceilings forming angles at the junctions, he recommends accordingly for the inside of his building, the form of a long oval, curved in every direction except that of the floor, placing a door at each end. By throwing open these doors, he seems to make it pretty apparent, that the smallest draught will be sufficient to effect an entire change in the whole stock of air; since at which ever end a current of air happens first to enter, it will carry all before it till it gets to the other. Opening windows, or other apertures, disposed in any other part of the room, would tend rather to disturb and counteract the current, than to promote it.

From the same reasoning it will follow, that the circular form demanded as the best of all by the inspection principle, must, in a view to ventilation, have in a considerable degree the advantage over *rectilinear;* and even, were the difference sufficiently material, the inspection principle might be applied to his oval with little or no disadvantage. The form of the inspection lodge might in this case follow that of the containing building; and that central part, so far from obstructing the ventilation, would rather, as it should seem, assist it, increasing the force of the current by the compressure.

It should seem also, that to a circular building, the central lodge would thus give the same aptitude to ventilation, which the Doctor's oval form possesses of itself.

To save his patients from catching cold while the current is passing through the room, the Doctor allows to each a short *screen*, like the head of a cradle, to be rested on the bed.

Here the use of the tin *speaking-tubes* would be seen again, in the means they would afford to the patient, though he were equal to no more than a whisper, of conveying to the lodge the most immediate notice of his wants, and receiving answers in a tone equally unproductive of disturbance.

Something I could have wished to say on the important difference between the general and comparatively immaterial impurity resulting merely from the *phlogiston*, and the various particular impurities constituted by the various products of *putrefaction*, or by the different matters of the various *contagions*. Against these very different dangers, the mode and measure of precaution might admit of no small difference. But this belongs not necessarily to the subject, and you would not thank me, any more than gentlemen of the faculty who understand it better than I, or gentlemen at large who would not wish to understand it.

An hospital built and conducted upon a plan of this kind, of the success of which everybody might be an observer, accessible to the patients' friends, who, without incommoding or being incommoded, might see the whole economy of it carried on under their eye, would lose, it is to be hoped, a great part of those repelling terrors, which deprive of the benefit of such institutions many objects whom prejudice, in league with poverty, either debars altogether from relief, or drives to seek it in much less eligible shapes. Who knows but that the certainty of a medical attendance, not occasional, short-lived, or even precarious, as at present, but constant and uninterrupted, might not render such a situation preferable even to home, in the eyes of many persons who could afford to pay for it? and that the erection of a building of this kind might turn to account in the hands of some enterprising practitioner?

A *prison*, as I observed in a former letter includes an hospital. In prisons on this construction, every cell may receive the properties of an hospital, without undergoing any change. The whole prison would be perhaps a better hospital than any building known hitherto by that name. Yet should it be thought of use, a few cells might be appropriated to that purpose; and perhaps it may be thought advisable that some cases of infection should be thrown out, and lodged under another roof.

But if infection in general must be sent to be cured elsewhere, there is no spot in which infection originating in negligence can, either in the *rise* or *spread* of it, meet with such obstacles as here. In what other instance as in this, will you see the interests of the governor and the governed in this important particular, so perfectly confounded and made one?—those of the keeper with those of the prisoners—those of the medical curator with those of the patients? Clean or unclean, safe or unsafe, he runs the chance that they do: if he lets them poison themselves, he lets them poison him. Encompassed on all sides by a multitude of persons, whose good or bad condition depends upon himself, he stands as a hostage in his own hands for the salubrity of the whole.

== Letter XXI.: Schools. == After applying the inspection principle first to prisons, and through mad-houses bringing it down to hospitals, will the parental feelings endure my applying it at last to schools? Will the observation of its efficacy in preventing the irregular application of undue hardship even to the guilty, be sufficient to dispel the apprehension of its tendency to introduce tyranny into the abodes of innocence and youth?

Applied to these, you will find it capable of two very distinguishable degrees of extension:—It may be confined to the hours of study; or it may be made to fill the whole circle of time, including the hours of repose, and refreshment, and recreation.

To the first of these applications the most captious timidity, I think, could hardly fancy an objection: concerning the hours of study, there can, I think, be but one wish, that they should be employed in study. It is scarce necessary to observe that gratings, bars, and bolts, and every circumstance from which an inspection-house can derive a terrific character, have nothing to do here. All play, all chattering—in short, all distraction of every kind, is effectually banished by the central and covered situation of the master, seconded by partitions or screens between the scholars, as slight as you please. The different measures and casts of talent, by this means rendered, perhaps for the first time, distinctly discernible, will indicate the different degrees of attention and modes of culture most suitable to each particular disposition; and incurable and irreproachable dulness or imbecility will no longer be punished for the sins of idleness or obstinacy. That species of fraud at Westminster called cribbing, a vice thought hitherto congenial to schools, will never creep in here. That system of premature corruption, in which idleness is screened by opulence, and the honour due to talents or industry is let out for hire, will be completely done away; and a nobleman may stand as good a chance of knowing something as a common man.

Nor, in point of present enjoyment, will the scholars be losers by the change. Those sinkings of the heart at the thoughts of a task undone, those galling struggles between the passion for play and the fear of punishment, would there be unknown. During the hours of business, habit, no longer broken in upon by accident, would strip the master's presence of its terrors, without depriving it of its use. And the time allotted for study being faithfully and rigidly appropriated to that service, the less of it would serve.

The separate spaces allotted for this purpose would not in other respects be thrown away. A bed, a bureau, and a chair, must be had at any rate; so that the only extraordinary expense in building would be for the *partitions,* for which a very slight thickness would suffice. The youth of either sex might by this means sleep, as well as study, under inspection, and alone—a circumstance of no mean importance in many a parent's eye.

In the Royal Military School at Paris, the bed-chambers (if my brother's memory does not deceive him) form two ranges on the two sides of a long room; the inhabitants being separated from one another by *partitions,* but exposed alike to the view of a master at his walks, by a kind of a *grated window* in each door. This plan of construction struck him, he tells me, a good deal, as he walked over that establishment (about a dozen years ago, was it not?) with you; and possibly in that walk the foundation was laid for his Inspection-House. If he there borrowed his idea, I hope he has not repaid it without interest. You will confess some difference, in point of facility, betwixt a state of incessant walking and a state of rest; and in point of completeness of inspection, between visiting two or three hundred persons one after another, and seeing them at once.

In stating what this principle *will* do in promoting the progress of instruction in every line, a word or two will be thought sufficient to state what it will *not* do. It *does* give every degree of efficacy which can be given to the influence of *punishment* and *restraint.* But it does nothing towards correcting the oppressive influence of panishment and restraint, by the enlivening and invigorating influence of *reward.* That noblest and brightest engine of discipline can by no other means be put to constant use in schools, than by the practice which at Westminster, you know, goes by the name of *challenging*—an institution which, paying merit in its fittest and most inexhaustible coin, and even uniting in one impulse the opposite powers of reward and punishment, holds out dishonour for every attention a boy omits, and honour for every exertion he can bestow.

With regard to the extending the range of inspection over every moment of a boy's time, the sentiments of mankind might not be altogether so unanimous. The notion, indeed, of most parents is, I believe, that children cannot be too much under the master's eye; and if man were a consistent animal, none who entertain that notion but should be fonder of the principle the farther they saw it pursued. But as consistency is of all human qualities the most rare, it need not at all surprise us, if, of those who in the present state of things are most anxious on the head of the master's omnipresence, many were to fly back and change their note, when they saw that point screwed up at once to a pitch of perfection so much beyond whatever they could have been accustomed to conceive.

Some there are, at any rate, who, before they came into so novel a scheme, would have many scruples to get over. Doubts would be started—Whether it would be advisable to apply such constant and unremitting pressure to the tender mind, and to give such herculean and ineludible strength to the gripe of power?—whether persons, of the cast of character and extent of ideas that may be expected to be found in the common run of schoolmasters, are likely to be fit receptacles for an authority so much exceeding anything that has been hitherto signified by *despotic?*—whether the *in*-attention of the master may not be as necessary to the *present* comfort of his *pupil,* in some respects, as the attention of the one may be to the *future* welfare of the other, in other respects?—whether the irretrievable check given to the free development of the intellectual part of his frame by this unintermitted pressure, may not be productive of an imbecility similar to that which would be produced by constant and long-continued *bandages* on the corporeal part?—whether what is thus acquired in *regularity* may not be lost in *energy?*—whether that not less instructive, though less heeded, course of discipline, which in the struggles of passion against passion, and of reason against reason, is administered by the children to one another and to themselves, and in which the conflicts and competitions that are to form the business of maturity are rehearsed in miniature; whether I say, this moral and most important branch of instruction would not by these means be sacrificed to the rudiments, and those seldom the most useful, of the intellectual?—whether the defects, with which *private* education has been charged in its comparison with public, would not here be carried to the extreme?—and whether, in being made a little better acquainted with the world of abstraction than they might have been otherwise, the youth thus pent up may not have been kept more than proportionably ignorant of the world of realities into which they are about to launch?—whether the liberal spirit and energy of a free citizen would not be exchanged for the mechanical discipline of a soldier, or the austerity of a monk?—and whether the result of this high-wrought contrivance might not be constructing a set of *machines* under the similitude of *men?*

To give a satisfactory answer to all these queries, which are mighty fine, but do not any of them come home to the point, it would be necessary to recur at once to the end of education. Would *happiness* be most likely to be increased or diminished by this discipline?—Call them soldiers, call them monks, call them machines: so they were but happy ones, I should not care. Wars and storms are best to rid of, but peace and calms are better to enjoy. Don't be frightened now, my dear * * * * *, and think that I am going to entertain you with a course of moral philosophy, or even with a system of education. Happiness is a very pretty thing to feel, but very dry to talk about; so you may unknit your brow, for I shall say no more about the matter. One thing only I will add, which is, that whoever sets up an inspection-school upon the tiptop of the principle, had need to be very sure of the master; for the boy's body is not more the child of his father's, than his mind will be of the master's mind; with no other difference than what there is between *command* on one side and *subjection* on the other.

Some of these fine queries which I have been treating you with, and finer still, Rousseau would have entertained us with; nor do I imagine he would have put his *Emilius* into an inspection-house; but I think he would have been glad of such a school for his Sophia.

Addison, the grave and moral Addison, in his *Spectator* or his *Tatler*, I forget which, suggests a contrivance for trying *virginity* by means of *lions*. You may there find many curious disquisitions concerning the measures and degrees of that species of purity; all which you will be better pleased to have from that grave author than from me. But, without plunging into any such discussions, the highest degree possible, whatsoever that may be, is no more than anybody might make sure of, only by transferring damsels at as early an age as may be thought sufficient, into a strict inspection-school. Addison's scheme was not only a penal but a bloody one: and what havoc it might have made in the population of the country, I tremble but to think of. Give thanks, then, to *Diana* and the *eleven thousand virgins,* and to whatever powers preside over virginity in either *calendar,* for so happy a discovery as this of your friend's. There you saw blood and uncertainty: here you see certainty without blood. What advantage might be made by setting up a boarding-school for young ladies upon this plan, and with what eagerness gentlemen who are curious in such matters would crowd to such a school to choose themselves wives, is too obvious to insist on. The only inconvenience I can think of is, that if the institution were to become general, Mrs. Ch. H. and other gentlewomen of her calling, would be obliged either to give up house-keeping, or take up with low wenches or married ladies.

Dr. Brown the estimator would have been stark mad for an inspection-school upon the very extremity of the principle, provided always he were to have been head-master, and then he would have had no other schools but those. His antagonist, Dr. Priestly, would, I imagine, be altogether as averse to it, unless, perhaps, for experiment's sake, upon a small scale, just enough to furnish an appendix to *Hartley upon Man.*

You have a controversy, I find, in England, about Sunday-schools. Schools upon the extremity of the inspection-principle would, I am apt to think, find more advocates among the patrons than among the oppugners of that measure.

We are told, somewhere or other, of a King of Egypt (*Psammitichus,* I think, is his name) who thinking to re-discover the lost original of language, contrived to breed up two children in a sequestered spot, secluded, from the hour of their birth, from all converse with the rest of humankind. No great matters were, I believe, collected from this experiment. An inspection-house, to which a set of children had been consigned from their birth, might afford experiments enough that would be rather more interesting. What say you to a *foundling-hospital* upon this principle? Would * * * *'s *manes* give you leave to let your present school and build another upon this ground? If I do not misrecollect, your brethren in that trust have gone so far as to make a point, where it can be effected, of taking the children out of the hands of their parents as much as possible, and even, if possible, altogether. If you have gone thus far, you have passed the Rubicon; you may even clap them up in an inspection-house, and then you make of them what you please. You need never grudge the parents *a peep behind the curtain* in the master's lodge. There, as often as they had a mind, they might see their children thriving and learning, if that would satisfy them, without interrupting business or counteracting discipline. Improving upon Psammitichus's experiment, you might keep up a sixteen or eighteen years separation between the male and female part of your young subjects; and at the end of that period see what the language of love would be, when *Father Francis's Ganders* were turned into *Father Francis's Geese.*

I know who would have been delighted to set up an inspection-school, if it were only for the experiment's sake, and that is Helvetius: at least, if he had been steady to his principles, which he was said to be: for by that contrivance, and by that alone, he might have been enabled to give an experimental proof of the truth of his position (supposing it to be true) that anybody may be taught anything, one person as well as another. It would have been his fault, if what he requires as a condition, viz. that the subjects of the experiment be placed in circumstances exactly similar, were not fulfilled.

A rare field for discovery in *metaphysics:* a science which, now for the first time, may be put to the test of experiment, like any other. Books, conversation, sensible objects, everything, might be *given.* The genealogy of each observable idea might be traced through all its degrees with the utmost nicety: the parent stocks being all known and numbered. Party men, controversialists of every description, and all other such epicures, whose mouth waters at the mammon of power, might here give themselves a rich treat, adapted to their several tastes, unembittered by contradiction. Two and two might here be less than four, or the moon might be made of green cheese; if any pious founder, who were rich enough, chose to have her of that material. Surrounded by a circle of pupils, obsequious beyond anything as yet known under the name of obsequiousness, their happiness might in such a mansion be complete, if any moderate number of adherents could content them; which unhappily is not the case. At the end of some twenty or five-and-twenty years, introduce the scholars of the different schools to one another (observing first to tie their hands behind them) and you will see good sport; though perhaps you may think there is enough of that kind of sport already. But if you throw out this hint to anybody, you will take care, as far as sects and religions are concerned, not to mention names; for of these, how few are there but would be ready to pull us to pieces, if they saw their rivals set down upon the same line, as candidates for the same advantage? And this is what we should get by our impartiality.—You may, however, venture to hint, that the money which is now laid out for propagating controversy, by founding sermons and lectures, might be laid out with greater certainty of advantage in the founding *controversial inspection-schools*. The preachers must be sad bunglers, indeed, if they had not there as many adherents as auditors; which is not always the case in the world at large. As to flagellation, and other such ceremonies, which more through custom than necessity are used by way of punishment in schools, but which under some institutions form the *routine* of life, I need not take up your time in showing how much the punctuality of those transactions might, in the latter case, be improved by the inspection principle. These monastic accomplishments have not been in fashion in our country for some ages:—therefore it would be lost labour to recommend the principle in that view. Neither are they a whit more so where I write; so that I should get as little thanks for my pains, were I to make such a proposal here. On the contrary, we are dissolving monasteries as you would lumps of sugar. A lump, for instance, we got the other day at Kieff, enough to feed a brace of regiments, besides pickings for other people. But if in my return to England, or at any other time, I should happen to go by the monastery of *La Trappe*, or any other where they are in earnest about such business, it would be cruelty to deny them the assistance it might be made to receive from the inspection principle. *Flinching* would then be as impracticable in a monastery, as cribbing in a school. Old scores might thus be rubbed out with as much regularity as could be desired; nor would the pride of Toboso have been so long a-disenchanting, could her *Knight* have put his coward *Squire* into an inspection-house.

Panopticon; or, The Inspection-House

Neither do I mean to give any instructions to the Turks for applying the inspection principle to their *seraglios:* no, not though I were to go through Constantinople again twenty times, notwithstanding the great saving it would make in the article of *eunuchs*, of whom one trusty one in the inspection-lodge would be as good as half a hundred. The price of that kind of cattle could not fail of falling at least ten per cent., and the insurance upon marital honour at least as much, upon the bare hint given of such an establishment in any of the Constantinople papers. But the mobbing I got at *Shoomlo.* only for taking a peep at the town from a thing they call a *minaret* (like our monument) in pursuance of invitation, has cancelled any claims they might have had upon me for the dinner they gave me at the divan, had it been better than it was.

If the idea of some of these applications should have brought a smile upon your countenance, it won't hurt you, my dear * * * *; nor should it hurt the principle. Your candour will prevent you from condemning a great and new invented instrument of government, because some of the purposes to which it is possible to apply it may appear useless, or trifling, or mischievous, or ridiculous. Its great excellence consists in the great strength it is capable of giving to *any* institution it may be thought proper to apply it to. If any perverse applications should ever be made of it, they will lie in this case as in others, at the doors of those who make them. Knives, however sharp, are very useful things, and, for most purposes, the sharper the more useful. I have no fear, therefore, of your wishing to forbid the use of them, because they have been sometimes employed by school-boys *to raise the devil* with, or by assassins to cut throats with.

I hope no critic of more learning than candour will do an inspection-house so much injustice as to compare it to *Dionysius' ear.* The object of that contrivance was, to know what prisoners said without their suspecting any such thing. The object of the inspection principle is directly the reverse: it is to make them not only *suspect*, but be *assured*, that whatever they do is known, even though that should not be the case. Detection is the object of the first: *prevention*, that of the latter. In the former case the ruling person is a spy; in the latter he is a monitor. The object of the first was to pry into the secret recesses of the heart; the latter, confining its attention to *overt* acts, leaves thoughts and fancies to their proper *ordinary*, the court *above.*

When I consider the extensive variety of purposes to which this principle may be applied, and the certain efficacy which, as far as I can trust my own conceptions, it promises to them all, my wonder is, not only that this plan should never have hitherto been put in practice, but how any other should ever have been thought of.

In so many edifices, as, from the time of the conquest to the present, have been built for the express purpose of safe custody, does it sound natural that, instead of placing the prisoners under the inspection of their keepers, the one class should have been lodged at one end, perhaps, of a vast building, and the other at another end?— as if the object of the establishment were, that those who wished to escape might carry on their schemes in concert, and at leisure. I should suppose the inspection principle must long ago have occurred to the ingenious, and been rejected by the judicious, could I, after all my efforts, conceive a reason for the rejection. The circular form, notwithstanding its taking demonstrably less materials than any other, may, for aught I know, on its first construction, be more expensive than one of equal dimensions in any of the ordinary forms. But this objection, which has no other source than the loose and random surmise of one who has had no experience in building, can never have held good in comparison with all the other prisons that we have, if in truth it holds good in comparison with any. Witness the massy piles of Newgate, of which the enormous, and upon the common plans by no means unnecessary expense, has been laid out in the purchase of a degree of security, not equal to that which the circular form would have given to the slightest building that could be made to hold together. In short, as often as I indulge myself in the liberty of fancying that my own notions on this head may prove conformable to other people's, I think of the old story of *Columbus* and his *egg.*

I have now set this *egg* of ours on its end:—whether it will stand fast, and bear the shocks of discussion, remains to be decided by experience. I think you will not find it stale; but its freshness is a circumstance, that may not give it an equal relish to every palate.

What would you say, if by the gradual adoption and diversified application of this single principle, you should see a new scene of things spread itself over the face of civilized society?—morals reformed, health preserved, industry invigorated, instruction diffused, public burthens lightened, economy seated as it were upon a rock, the gordian knot of the poor-laws not cut but untied—all by a simple idea in architecture?

I am, &c.

Lightning Source UK Ltd.
Milton Keynes UK
05 February 2010

149651UK00001B/31/P